TARP TOWN U S A

Other works by D T Pollard

**Rooftop Diva – A Novel of Triumph
After Katrina (fiction)**

**Fools' Heaven – Love, Lust and
Death Beyond the Pulpit (fiction)**

TARP Town U S A

The Recession That Saved America

D T Pollard

Book Express

Copyright © 2009 by Danny T. Pollard

Book Express Books may be ordered through
booksellers or by contacting

Book Express
P.O. Box 541651
Grand Prairie, TX 75052
www.DTPollard.com
dtpollard@dtpollard.com

This is a work of non-fiction
isbn: 978-0-9824606-0-3 (pbk)
isbn: 978-0-9824606-1-0 (ebk)
.
First Printing

Printed in the United States of America

This book is dedicated to everyone trying to better their lives while living in TARP Town U S A.

INTRODUCTION

♦

TARP Town U S A is an inspiration that came to me after witnessing and living in the midst of the recession that started in the United States in 2007. The explosion of shocking financial revelations during the last quarter of 2008 initiated a series of actions that had never been witnessed in this country before. Even the course of the Presidential election was altered by the unexpected turn of events.

I am a citizen of this great country and have lived long enough to experience a metamorphosis in how this nation operates. The circumstances that led to the unraveling of our economy, banking system and housing market was an expression of the exercise of unbridled greed and lax oversight of our financial markets.

I am a writer and this is my vision of how I saw and felt what was taking place. Hardworking individuals who built this great republic with their heart, heads and hands experienced the greatest downfall as the middle class appeared to be systematically dismantled.

The unrestrained pursuit of wealth by a select few served to harm many more. The greatest upward wealth transfer in the history of this country left a trail of destruction that is still being calculated.

D T Pollard

Chapter 1

♦

On September 22, 2008, I reached the age of 50 years old. Less than one month later the United States, as I knew it, ceased to exist. An economic collapse caused by unbridled Wall-Street greed transformed pockets of the nation into concrete wastelands and tent cities that I refer to as TARP Town U S A.

As an American citizen and the son of common laborers, my destiny was intertwined with the fate of the nation. My father farmed the earth and my mother's jobs ranged from pulling cotton to toiling in sewing factories. Coming out of small rural east Texas community, I managed to attain a level of education and a lifestyle they never experienced. In many ways my parents were the people who lived the true American dream and raised nine children with labor, heart and love. When my mother and father left this earth together in a tragic vehicle accident in 1985, they owed no man or institution. The simple frame house where I grew up to adulthood was free and clear of any liens or attachments as was the one acre of land it sat on. Actually, most of my family and neighbors lived in a similar manner which was considered quite normal for that time and place. Straightforward people who had little in terms of material wealth or pretension surrounded me. My parents often told us, as long as you owned your own home, you always had a place to rest your head if everything else in life failed.

Throughout history a great nation called the United States of America beamed as a beacon to the rest of the world. For hundreds of years, souls yearning for freedom risked death striving to reach her shores in pursuit of the promise of a better life. All men are created equal, was the creed of this new republic. Somewhere in history some men became elevated above the masses and ushered in the era of the gods of greed. That once powerful light of freedom is flickering and the jury is out on whether it will be extinguished or once again shines brighter than ever before.

The ability to achieve greatness regardless of your birth circumstances gave Americans the will to rise every morning and toil, often in harsh conditions, to provide for their families. A man with nothing more than the strength of his back and will to work could secure his place among the dignified as he contributed to building a nation. The sweat from his brow was rewarded with the means to obtain food, shelter and security for his family. Many labored in dangerous conditions far below the earth extracting coal to power the nation and yes, some gave their lives. Others farmed the land to provide food to the masses. Another group took sacred oaths and patrolled in distant lands engaging hostile forces. Thousands have died in the course of fulfilling their duty and did so with honor. The greatness of this country has been sorely tested over the years. Men, women and children rose from bondage to make their own claim on the dream of the country's founding fathers. Women added to the country's foundation with their heads, hands and hearts to make sure this nation lived up to its potential. All across this vast landscape in the air, on land and at sea, Americans made sacrifices that added to the vitality of this country and kept it alive.

Those who excelled in their assignments could secure their piece of the American dream and own a home of their own. By being dutiful with their treasure, honoring their debts and setting something aside for providence it was possible to move into the category of home ownership. There was something special when someone could say, 'I own my own home'. The pride would jump from their chest because becoming a homeowner has always been a special rite of passage in a free society.

Although some would be able to qualify and enter into a home ownership contract, others would fall short of the requirements and still had to rent places of inhabitance. Some were simply careless with their finances or uncontrollable circumstances caused them to fall short of credit worthiness standards. There was a vast pool of people who were not making home loan payments although they were still generating a huge currency flow by paying monthly rental obligations.

Temptation has always occupied a seat at the table of the money changers on Wall Street in New York City. Wall Street is where the temple of financial exchange resides in America. Somehow the elected representatives voters sent to Washington D.C. became enabling agents in what became the greatest wealth transfer from the populace in the history of the United States. That circumstance and the resulting fallout threatened to plunge the world into a global financial abyss.

While chaos edged closer, the captains of finance and other industries had stored up great wealth extracted from the huddled masses. Investment bank executives gazed out from their cavernous walnut-wood-lined enclaves perched high above the earth below and planned their next moves. It became the cruelest of ironies as the working class would ultimately depend upon those who inflicted harm upon them to be their saviors. It was difficult to determine if individuals had benevolent or sinister motives, you could only judge their actions.

On October 3, 2008, the United States House of Representative authorized the use $700 billion of the taxpayers' money to relieve fiscal constipation caused by years of sociopathic financial behavior. The gods of greed had consumed the succulent core of wealth from the American populace like an invasive parasite. The resulting toxic waste byproduct threatened to plunge the country and world into another Great Depression.

This authorized robbery was so brazen and bold that I had to admire the process as I abhorred the act. All of the great criminal capers in history paled by comparison. Not Billy the Kid, Al Capone, Bonnie and Clyde, Mafia, drug cartels or any other unlawful enterprise known to man came close to this level of ruthless efficiency. In one fell swoop, 300 million Americans were legally robbed in mass.

I watched in amazement as a loaded financial gun was held to the temple of Congress. The House of Representatives played Russian roulette and spun the gun cylinder. The financial rescue bill failed to pass on the first round of voting. The stock market pulled the trigger and fired a shot heard across the the country as the Dow Jones Industrial Average dropped 777 points after the rescue bill failed. With the message delivered loud and clear, the Senate swung into action, took up the bill and passed their version of the rescue package for the House to consider later. The rest is or will be history.

I don't know what the future holds but I will never forget how a nation's treasure was plundered to enrich a select few using the greatest lure of all, the desire to own a home of your own. Exactly how did this happen? What caused an incoming President to assume office wearing financial handcuffs as the next commander in chief? How did a lame-duck Secretary of Treasury, Henry Paulson, formerly the head of the investment bank Goldman Sachs, position himself to ask for a $700 billion blank check with a three-page written plan? Paulson's plan would have given him unquestionable and irrevocable authority over how those funds were used. Congress rejected Paulson's plan and came up with an alternative. This was a tragedy beyond measure for future generations and for those with little understanding of what pushed us to the brink of financial ruin. This was the ultimate inside job.

Multi-million dollar CEO payouts that paid whether their companies performed profitably or not and insane profits from multiple sales of mortgaged backed securities encouraged Wall Street to engage in a drunken money orgy. Then the hangover hit. After hanging out at the bar of financial irresponsibility until the entire stock of prime grade libations had been consumed, the American taxpayers were asked to pick up the tab.

This was not the act of a single sociopath, but of a rare sociopathic system. Like most pyramid schemes it starts with the ground level. The ground level in this case consisted of homeowners and those desiring to be homeowners. A cornerstone of the American dream is to own a home of your own. The classic way to purchase a home was to go to a bank, prove your credit worthiness, have enough savings for a down payment and demonstrate a solid ability to satisfy the mortgage payments. The bank made its profit by holding the note until maturity for the full 15 or 30 years and collected the interest. Both parties bore substantial risk and responsibility.

Home mortgages were boring, sleepy and long term profit financial instruments. Mortgages also represented the largest single purchase an individual would usually make during their lifetime. The unique characteristic separating mortgages from other consumer loans was a desire of almost everyone to obtain one. The simple reason was because a mortgage represented home ownership. Owning your own home meant you had attained the ultimate in securing your family's security and legacy. You became **"somebody"** when you owned your own home.

Stocks, bonds and commodities were a different breed. Trading in those investments formed the foundation of our financial exchange markets. Stocks represented equity in companies. Bonds were debt instruments to raise capital with longer term payoffs. Commodities were real goods such as oil, precious metals and food products. Those instruments represented the hot, fashionable and sophisticated side of things in the financial sector.

Mortgages were the quiet wallflowers of financial products. Home mortgages were retail products utilized by average individuals striving to attain the goal of home ownership. Wrapped up in restrictive regulations, home loans required several tests of financial stability on the part of borrowers before they could qualify for a 15 to 30 year debt commitment. They were slow, conservative and not trendy like flashier items such as stocks. Mortgages also represented a massive financial cash flow in the form of collective monthly payments.

Financial managers eyed an enormous pool of renters like a purveyor of human flesh viewed a vulnerable individual. The question was simple. How could they co-opt that cash-flow for their gain? The targets were standing in plain sight, the huge group of people who could not meet the requirements to qualify for a conventional home loan. Like any pimp worthy of his profession, all it took was the right angle.

After the stranger sat at the bar next to his intended target he baited the hook and dangled it in front of his intended victim.

"Look, I've got something you can't resist. You too, can own a home of your own," the stranger said while looking around to see if anyone was watching.

"I've tried already. I don't qualify," was the dejected reply.

"Hey man, I know where you're coming from. I've got some new stuff to drop on you. Let me show you how it works."

The stranger pulled a stack of papers from a black bag and spread them out across the bar and proceeded to describe the various options to the stunned individual.

"Look, you've never seen anything like this before, this stuff is primo. This is a one-hundred-percent finance deal. Now this one is called a pick-a-payment loan. You know, if you get in a squeeze one month, just pay the interest. This is a hot one; it's called an adjustable rate mortgage. You pay less for a few years and then it goes up later. There are jumbo loans, balloon notes, you name it and I've got it."

"I've tried already. I still wouldn't qualify."

"That's where the twist comes in. This is a new world called subprime mortgages. It was made with you in mind. You deserve a nice home just like everybody else. Just because you had a couple of bad breaks in the past shouldn't keep you from owning a home of you own, how about it?"

The stunned individual hesitated for a second, then he took a pen from the stranger, filled out an application and the game was on. The news of those new subprime mortgages spread like wildfire. Mortgage brokers, real estate agents, subprime lenders, real estate speculators and others came out of the woodwork. Some people were professionals and others were opportunists seeking to cash in during the feeding frenzy. Banks and mortgage companies quickly established subprime mortgage divisions in order to compete in this lucrative new segment of home lending. The modern-day equivalent of the gold rush ensued. Tract homebuilders were barely able to keep up with the explosion in demand. Developers transformed previously neglected expanses of land into master-planned bedroom communities from coast to coast. Much of that new bounty came from those least likely to sustain their newly elevated lifestyles and financial responsibilities. The CEO's of Wall Street looked out across the land at what they had created and determined it was good.

Since the captains of finance had found a way to tap into the vast amounts of money represented by home mortgages, they transformed them into tradable financial products. In effect the mortgage was disconnected from the homes they represented and sold as a new type of debt security. After the lowly mortgage was liberated from the homes they financed, it was time to transform them from ugly ducklings into irresistible financial products. The finishing touch was to give a new identity to this new star on the horizon. It had to be provocative, how about mortgage backed securities? Two other things were needed to seal the deal, credibility and low risk. Credibility came from trusted credit agencies deeming these financial instruments good credit risks. Default concerns were satisfied by the creation of a quasi-insurance policy called a credit default swap. Don't worry; in case something happens, you can purchase a money-back-guarantee, the only problem was no one bothered to verify if assets existed to back those guarantees.

In order to bring these complex arrangements into clearer focus is the following illustration from the FDIC:

Statement of Sheila C. Bair, Chairman, Federal Deposit Insurance Corporation on Possible Responses to Rising Mortgage Foreclosures before the Committee on Financial Services, U.S. House of Representatives; 2128 Rayburn House Office Building April 17, 2007

Borrowing Under the Traditional Borrower/Lender Relationship

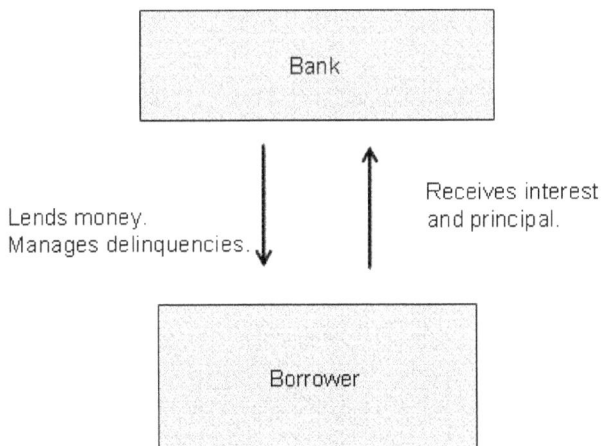

```
                  ┌────────────────────┐
                  │        Bank        │
                  └────────────────────┘
                        │      ↑
Lends money.            │      │     Receives interest
Manages delinquencies. ↓      │     and principal.
                  ┌────────────────────┐
                  │      Borrower      │
                  └────────────────────┘
```

The securitization structure diagram that follows shows the components of a typical securitization. It is important to note that not all securitizations are identical. For example, the lender and the servicer are sometimes the same entity, or in other arrangements brokers may not play a role. Nevertheless, the diagram generally illustrates the roles of the various participants in a securitization structure.

Borrowing Under a Securitization Structure

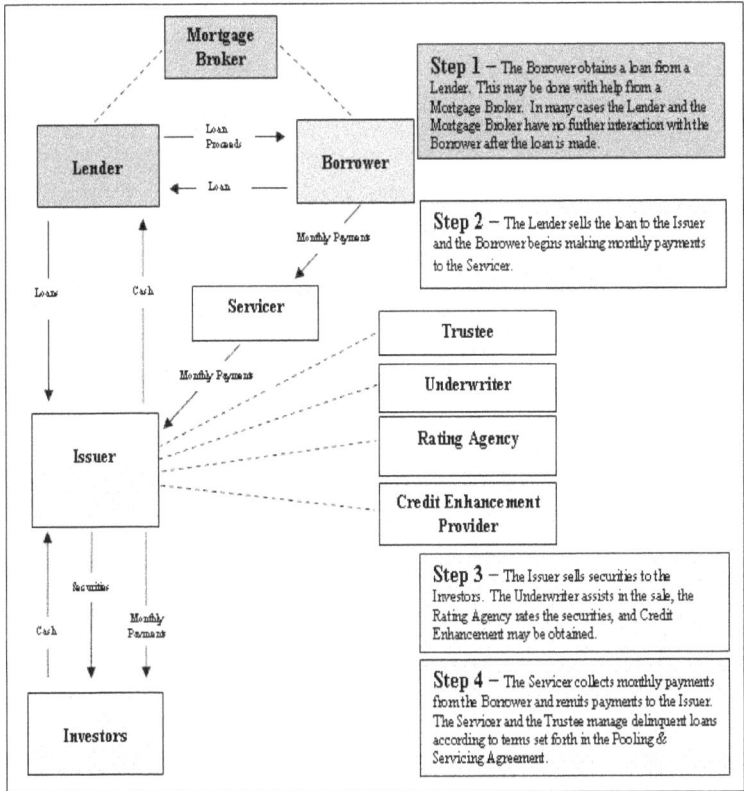

Step 1 – The Borrower obtains a loan from a Lender. This may be done with help from a Mortgage Broker. In many cases the Lender and the Mortgage Broker have no further interaction with the Borrower after the loan is made.

Step 2 – The Lender sells the loan to the Issuer and the Borrower begins making monthly payments to the Servicer.

Step 3 – The Issuer sells securities to the Investors. The Underwriter assists in the sale, the Rating Agency rates the securities, and Credit Enhancement may be obtained.

Step 4 – The Servicer collects monthly payments from the Borrower and remits payments to the Issuer. The Servicer and the Trustee manage delinquent loans according to terms set forth in the Pooling & Servicing Agreement.

As the terminology is used in the securitization contracts and in the diagram above, the key elements to a typical securitization include the following:

- **Issuer** - A bankruptcy-remote special purpose entity (SPE) formed to facilitate

21

a securitization and to issue securities to investors.[8]

- **Lender** - An entity that underwrites and funds loans that are eventually sold to the SPE for inclusion in the securitization. Lenders are compensated by cash for the purchase of the loan and by fees. In some cases, the lender might contract with mortgage brokers. Lenders can be banks or non-banks.

- **Mortgage Broker** - Acts as a facilitator between a borrower and the lender. The mortgage broker receives fee income upon the loan's closing.

- **Servicer** - The entity responsible for collecting loan payments from borrowers and for remitting these payments to the issuer for distribution to the investors. The servicer is typically compensated with fees based on the volume of loans serviced. The servicer is generally obligated to maximize the payments from the borrowers to the issuer, and is responsible for handling delinquent loans and foreclosures.

- **Investors** - The purchasers of the various securities issued by a securitization. Investors provide funding for the loans and assume varying degrees of credit risk, based on the terms of the securities they purchase.

- **Rating Agency** - Assigns initial ratings to the various securities issued by the issuer and updates these ratings based on subsequent performance and perceived risk. Rating agency criteria influence the initial structure of the securities.

- **Trustee** - A third party appointed to represent the investors' interests in a securitization. The trustee ensures that the securitization operates as set forth in the securitization documents, which may include determinations about the servicer's compliance with established servicing criteria.

- **Securitization Documents** - The documents create the securitization and specify how it operates. One of the securitization documents is the Pooling and Servicing Agreement (PSA), which is a contract that defines how loans will be combined in a securitization, the administration and servicing of the loans, representations and warranties, and permissible loss mitigation strategies that the servicer can perform in event of loan default.
- **Underwriter** - Administers the issuance of the securities to investors.
- **Credit Enhancement Provider** - Securitization transactions may include credit enhancement (designed to decrease the credit risk of the structure) provided by an independent third party in the form of letters of credit or guarantees.

Securitization takes the role of the lender and breaks it into separate components. Unlike the more traditional relationship between a borrower and a lender, securitization involves the sale of the loan by the lender to a new owner--the issuer--who then sells securities to investors. The investors are buying "bonds" that entitle them to a share of the cash paid by the borrowers on their mortgages. Once the lender has sold the mortgage to the issuer, the lender no longer has the power to restructure the loan or make other accommodations for its borrower. That becomes the responsibility of a servicer, who collects the mortgage payments, distributes them to the issuer for payment to investors, and, if the borrower cannot pay, takes action to recover cash for the investors. The servicer can only do what the securitization documents allow it to do. As described below, these contracts may constrain the servicer's flexibility to restructure the loans.

With so many parties and components involved, securitizations are significantly more complicated than the traditional borrower/lender relationship. The securitization is governed by securitization documents and is administered by a trustee. This separation of the functions previously done by a single lender creates a funding mechanism that has facilitated new types of financing and has expanded credit availability. However, the increased complexity of the structure and the different interests of the various securitization parties can make credit workout strategies more complicated than in a direct borrower/lender relationship.

The interests and obligations of the various parties are set forth in the securitization documents and are closely monitored by the trustee. Further complicating the situation is the fact that the interests of the participants might not be aligned – with each other or with the borrower. Generally speaking, this arrangement complicates the loan modification process.

Loan Restructuring Challenges

When difficulty arises in making payments on a securitized loan, the borrower generally will not be dealing with the local banker with whom there might be an established relationship. Instead, the

24

borrower will be dealing with a servicer. The servicer has responsibilities defined in the securitization documents that are substantially different than those of a lender. The servicer and the trustee are responsible for taking actions that are in the best interest of the investors who purchased portions of the securitization. Protecting the investors means determining the best alternative that would bring the maximum recovery on a defaulted loan on a present-value basis. If the servicer determines that a workout or modification of the loan achieves that goal, then there is an alignment of the investor/servicer/borrower relationship. However, if liquidation of the collateral (through a foreclosure or other means) results in the highest net present value of cash flows, the servicer may be bound by the terms of the securitization to pursue this approach to the benefit of the investor despite the resulting detriment to the borrower.

One piece missing from the diagram describing how mortgage backed security trading functioned was the item that caused AIG to have problems, the credit default swap. Add a block next to the one labeled Investors, connect them with a line and write credit default swap inside to represent where the CDS came into play. Credit default swaps were issued to insure investors against losses if the mortgage backed securities failed. An interesting fact about CDS transactions was the ability of parties, who had no interest in what the CDS was based on, to buy them on speculation of the referenced company going down or failing. For example someone could acquire a CDS with company X as the reference entity. If company X went down, the CDS paid out to the buyer, although the investor did not suffer any losses. What Wall Street called investing was called gambling in the real world.

Two occurrences created a tenuous environment for those mortgage backed securities. The lowering of credit standards, creation of easy entry mortgage products and low initial payment loans created a predictable explosion in the housing market. Homes moved from their primary function of simply being somewhere to live and became a game of how much house someone could acquire for the lowest payment. Secondly, homes became automatic teller machines with multiple refinancing opportunities as home values seemed to rise endlessly. Flipping houses became the new gold rush as purchase, rehab and resell became the new get-rich scheme for novice real estate investors. All was well as banks, investment banks, real estate firms, mortgage companies, mortgage brokers and exuberant new homeowners basked in the glow of what seemed to be a new golden age. It seemed this was an economic paradise.

The financial bonanza brought on by the boom in home mortgages was irresistible. Mortgages were cut, chopped, packaged and sold worldwide like kilos of cocaine as mortgage backed securities. The effect was just as addictive except those at the top mainlined dollars instead of drugs. Banks, investment banks and hedge fund managers were amassing huge fortunes. Unfortunately this Utopia was built upon a foundation of shifting sand. Those interest-only, adjustable-rate and balloon mortgages began to do what they must, demand payment for the actual value of the property financed.

Homebuyers now faced the reality of not being able to afford payments on a home costing, in some cases, double of what they could qualify for with conventional mortgage loan criteria. Some realized the multiple refinancing options they used to withdraw funds based upon a seemingly endless escalation of property values left them with a debt exceeding the value of the home. Sadly, others simply could not afford their house from the onset. The initial thought of refinancing into a fixed rate loan evaporated because they financed 100 percent of the home value. With no or negative equity in the home there was no way out for the homeowner financially.

The fall of the house of cards had begun. On the financial side there was a delayed effect. The boom in housing created a new kind of lucrative feeding frenzy in the financial markets that was destined to collapse. The bounty of home mortgages had been harvested and baled like hay in a vast field. Sadly the same bounty began to rot in the barns. These mortgage backed securities were sold multiple times over with each seller receiving a percentage from each successive new buyer. Investment banks and the fund managers involved reaped huge profits during the height of the housing boom.

As in most enterprises of this nature the end comes like a storm surge from an approaching hurricane. Pockets of disturbed activity could be detected in certain areas like California, Florida and Nevada where runaway home appreciation had fueled huge building booms, refinancing and speculation. The eye of this financial storm began to gain definition and alarms went off, but others downplayed the severity. One of the outer bands of the impending maelstrom landed a glancing blow in March 2008 as the 85-year-old investment bank Bear Sterns collapsed. Bear Sterns crumbled under pressure from something the general public was going to hear a lot more about, failed mortgage backed securities. Bear Sterns was sold to J P Morgan Chase. Then as if out of the blue another one of the mighty investment banks went down as Lehman Brothers failed in September 2008. The warning sirens went off full blast. The eye wall of this economic storm had landed and the financial levees failed. The federal government seized control of Fannie Mae and Freddie Mac. AIG, one of the largest insurance companies on earth buckled and was propped up with government assistance.

The CEOs of the American automakers, whose sales were battered by steep drops in demand, flew in on three separate private jets pleading poverty to congress while requesting bailouts. Citigroup was wheeled in on life support and received a multi-billion dollar government funds infusion while still vowing to spend $400 million on a baseball stadium branding transaction. As the parade of tragedy surrounded by lunacy continued. The people of the United States and the world watched in horror as the hard earned wealth of everyday citizens had been funneled upward and paid out as massive bonuses to a few at the top of the pyramid. The resulting wreckage from defaulted home loans and mortgage backed securities was described as toxic assets clogging up the financial system. Those were not toxic assets, but the collective rotting carcasses of the dashed dreams of millions of Americans. Like depleted oil fields, they were left to return to their prior state of existence.

I sat in silence as the new robber barons shoveled financial soil into the grave of what was once the greatest nation on earth. Nationwide, postmen were viewed like grim reapers as they delivered dire news in the form of devastating 401K statements that sent chills down the spines of individuals near retirement. Clearly, the economy of the United States of America had been kept alive by artificial means for years. After the financial steroids lost their effect, the country I loved had wasted away and was a shadow of its former self. Muscular shoulders once formed by a robust manufacturing sector had long since withered as many jobs were shipped out to lower cost labor centers around the world. A formerly vibrant brain was crippled by a gradual loss of replacement matter caused by a lessened emphasis on math and science in our education system. Science and high-technology talent was imported from around the globe. Even some of our most sensitive components for industrial, commercial and military applications were sourced from foreign firms. The United States will never be able to completely return to the glory years of the past, because that era has passed. We should be capable of forging a new reality based upon creating new areas in which to lead the world such as clean-energy technology creation.

In the midst of this madness, the United States of American crossed a bridge I thought I would not live to witness. A history of pain written in blood added a new chapter with the election of Barack Obama as the 44th President of the United States. A man of black African and white American decent became the chief executive of the country. A man with African and Anglo blood coursing through his veins attained the loftiest goal a child can have in this country. The world watched as the hope of a nation and the world exploded in celebration of a dream fulfilled as a new financial nightmare loomed. Welcome, Mr. President.

Chapter 2

♦

We quite often hear reports about a seemingly healthy person suddenly dying of some massive health failure. Usually upon closer examination there were obvious and unheeded warning signs. There was an eerie element of surprise amongst the general public when seemingly out of the blue the foundation fell from under our banking and investment community. In what must have felt like a bucket of cold water being thrown into the face of the average individual, we watched as multiple large corporations struggled for survival. The most frightening aspect of our sudden economic crisis was how oblivious everyone was that financial problems of that magnitude could develop with so little advance warning. Given the timing of the country's economic problems, it made for a stressful December, 2008 holiday season.

Sudden-unanticipated-failure is what we are asked to believed happened to the economy when decades-old banks, investment banks and an insurance giant all suffered a collective catastrophic event at the same time. It is unacceptable for anyone to accept explanations that experts on the inside never saw this coming.

From Wall Street to federal regulators, there has not been a rational report of why warnings were not sent out so preventative measures could have been taken instead of the financial triage that took place under most unfavorable circumstances.

In my view, financial executives who were pulling levers did not sound any warning bells until they drained every ounce of wealth before the patient died. If that was the case, then those people were beneath where even I had placed them. Knowingly allowing the economy to hemorrhage in silence would be a willful act of contempt towards the country and world. I can only hope the meltdown was an unlikely confluence of negative events. It seems to be ludicrous to believe individuals with high levels of expertise in their fields, such as the professionals managing huge investment banks, operated in ignorance.

As workers across the United States were turned out of their jobs by the hundreds of thousands monthly as a result of the recession, anger was building. Many in the world community were leveling blame on

America as the irresponsible actor that took the global economy down the road to ruin.

Fellow citizens looked on as images they thought they would never see in this nation unfolded before their eyes. In the United States of America, people were living outside in tent villages due to recent homelessness caused by an economic collapse. I have labeled those makeshift communities – TARP Towns. TARP is formed from the initials of the $700 billion Troubled Assets Relief Program which was created in October of 2008 to purchase failed mortgage related assets. I used the word TARP because while the banks were being bailed out, homeowners were being thrown out. When the first of these villages of displaced Americans was shown for the world to see, there was an audible gasp from the country, but an amazing lack of outrage. The term TARP Towns can also be extended to decimated cities and neighborhoods riddled with vacant homes due to foreclose.

In what must have felt like a never-ending nightmare, some residents living in makeshift communities were given eviction notices to move out of their tent cities. Americans were actually being evicted from homelessness. Could that be the beginning of a wandering band of citizens like we had during the Great Depression? Would TARP Towns become the new Hoovervilles?

Oddly enough the media coverage of tent cities that sprung up nationwide had been given relatively sparse national coverage. It could be a symptom of our story-of-the-minute driven media or an attempt to hide the real depth of pain this downturn has caused.

Chapter 3

♦

How did we get here? To know how this happened to the greatest economy on earth is really a reflection on how business and trade changed on a global scale over the last 50 years. Here is a news flash. The elevation of disconnected wealth over actual wealth is the primary problem. Let's examine exactly what disconnected wealth over actual wealth means in the context of the economic crisis of 2008 and 2009.

Disconnected wealth is simply the separation of financial output from the primary creation source. Separation is when the financial life of a creation source has an activity cycle totally separate from the source itself.

The creation of residential mortgage backed securities (MBS) was a perfect example of separation. Mortgage backed securities seemed to live in their own world and in many ways were Frankenstein products. MBS were basically bonds with yields based upon the stream of home loan payments. When these MBS were created, it was akin to a drug dealer cutting cocaine with baking soda. Mix in enough prime with subprime loans to make the bundle look attractive. The difference in this instance was the product was diluted before distribution to the street dealers, Wall Street traders, instead of after the fact. The cash flow that sustained those MBS was your monthly home mortgage payments. In fact a single mortgage may be involved in backing several MBS. Actually, the real value of the home itself had very little to do with the value of the resulting financial products which were sold worldwide. The home value ceased to matter because the original mortgage was no longer whole. In fact if it were not for home loan defaults interrupting the cash flow pool supporting mortgage backed securities (MBS), the current appraised value of the homes would have remained irrelevant. It was when the default levels of home loans hit a tipping point that caused the disconnected MBS to become a problem. Since everyone with a link to the sale or resale of those financial products received a percentage payout, it eventually had to track back to the original revenue source. The collateral securing those MBS was your home value and mortgage payments. The valued revenue source was the "magic" subprime loan the homeowner originally signed. Thus the sand began to shift under their new financial kingdom built upon the dreams of millions to satisfy long held desires to be the king or queen of their castle. In other words, the hoodwinking and bamboozling was uncovered for the world to see.

The meltdown in the financial markets and freezing of credit are really symptoms of self-inflicted wounds. Coincidently, many seemingly unrelated elements intersected to create a situation where we could fall and it would be questionable if we could ever get back up. To illustrate the problem, I have to go back to my childhood and look at the world through the eyes of a 10-year-old child in 1968.

I grew up in a small town where few people I knew went to college straight out of high school. It was simply not a requirement in order to live a good life. Many residents were able to do well by gaining employment at any number of well paying companies within a 40-mile radius. There were lumber mills, steel foundries, air-conditioner-assembly plants and many more. These enterprises were part of vertically integrated companies with most of the component parts originating from other parts of the United States. The America where anyone could learn a trade or work on an assembly line and achieve the reality of a proud middle-class lifestyle is a faded memory. Their dedication and hard labor reverberated throughout the land as the supply chain supported livelihoods nationwide. Those were the days when many products were sourced completely within the United States from raw materials to finished goods. The critical dimension of that lost world was the currency generated from the ultimate consumer of the product circulated many times over within our borders.

With a vertical currency flow dozens of locations nationwide were profit centers fed by one sales transaction. Vertical revenue flow supported payrolls in all of those communities and powered the economy. Fast forward to the future and the process had short circuited.

With modern global economics, manufacturing sources may be scattered around the globe with various components fabricated in different nations or continents. An automobile sold in the United States, but produced in Japan or Europe, only left the retailer profit in the country as the lion's share landed on foreign shores. Hold on, now we manufacture several foreign car models in the United States which is actually a troubling sign. It indicates our labor cost is low enough to offset the cost of manufacturing the vehicle elsewhere and shipping it to this country. The second alarm is it means enough vehicles are being sold to justify onshore plants to keep up with demand. Remember the bulk of the profit lands in another country. To be totally correct, the foreign automobile plants in the United States are assembly operations. American based foreign vehicle assembly plants bolt together subassemblies manufactured on a worldwide basis.

We have become a land of consumers, dependent on goods created in foreign lands. In a matter of a few decades the clarion call changed from "Made in the U.S.A." to "Everyday Low Prices", but at what real cost. We were all consumed in a race to a bottom with no end. It became apparent that the only way to continually lower the cost of various goods was to extract it out of the compensation paid to employees, in particular the manufacturing class. This was the beginning of the dismantling of the middle class who made this country great.

The devaluation of the worth of craftsmen, construction and factory workers increased with the onset of the information age and internet bubble. Seemingly, wealth could be created out of thin air. Combine a cutting edge concept with unique go to market web-based strategy and investors would line up to fund various ventures. Reality made an appearance when rational minds questioned how long it would be before actual profits would start to flow. Alas, another creation of the smartest people in the room exploded and paper fortunes disappeared into the electronic vapor they came from.

The genie of money-for-nothing never went away, but only continued to change the costume it wore. Two of its more interchangeable disguises over the last fifty years have been real estate paradises and financial wizardry. It was only a matter of time before the two joined in an unholy matrimony of ultimate greed. It was to be the perfect union of two fields with everything and nothing in common upon quick examination. Real estate was slow, sleepy and often wandered in the land of regular citizens. Home mortgages, commercial property development loans and their ilk were hardly financial instruments causing jet-setters to gasp in order to catch their breath.

Finance, stocks and bonds were much more the speed for Wall Street geniuses. Who had time to wait for a 15 or 30-year mortgage note to mature? Any hedge-fund manager or financial planner with any ambition at all planned to retire to one of several luxury hideaways within a few years of starting their careers. Wall Street enlisted mathematical wizards to create new products in financial laboratories which caused the often abused areas of real estate and financial trading to walk down the aisle together. Their union was one made in the kingdom of heavenly greed and excess. Never was a couple more supportive of each other and they achieved heights they could never reach as separate entities.

The dot.com bubble was an economic disaster, but it only served to hurt those chasing financial rainbows. Fleecing those wealthy enough to invest in fledgling internet ventures without receiving returns generated little sympathy from the general public. Enron was a different matter altogether. Enron was really one of the boldest corporate frauds in history and actually embodied a corporate criminal enterprise. Enron was a deceit encompassing fraudulent assets, accounting and manufactured earnings. Although there seemed to be similarities between what transpired with Enron and the mortgage backed security meltdown, one was criminal and the other was legal. The financial freefall of 2008 was triggered by a collapse of legally traded financial instruments.

Clearly those prior results failed to dig deep enough, they were devastating to the people affected but the scope of the damage was limited. There had to be a way to get to the financial bone and the nutritious marrow inside on a widespread basis so nothing would remain but the hollow hardened shell. The genius of the subprime loan/asset backed security union was a deep excavation into the financial depths of the middle and lower middle classes. Subprime lending allowed those previously unable to walk through the doors of home ownership to join the parade of sheep primed for financial sheering. People long denied the opportunity to bask in the pride of turning the key to enter the doorway they could call home, lined up willingly for what proved to be a time-released poison pill.

There was a period of apparent prosperity and it seemed that many had improved their lots in life. Block parties abounded as new neighbors greeted each other in their newly minted subdivisions. Over time there would be the spurious empty home going up for sale. Then the questions and whispers would begin regarding what happen to their neighbors who suddenly moved from the community. That was only the beginning of the end.

After the euphoria subsided and the mortgage foreclosures mounted, there were glazed stares and pointed fingers assigning blame. While there was enough fraud, greed and abuse to go around, the money was gone. Investors clutched at worthless promises in the form of the previously mentioned quasi-insurance policies called credit default swaps, which turned out to be backed by not much more than the paper they were written on. Now it seemed to be time for a contentious divorce and swift settlement with a $700 billion taxpayer-backed good faith payment as a start. Of course Wall Street wanted to dump the full cost for its messy marriage dissolution onto someone else without losing anything it brought into the union. As this divorce drama played out, it seemed the fallout from untangling the affairs of those two toxic paramours was causing widespread destruction and the shrapnel hit almost every sector of the economy. Credit markets were blocked, the housing market was collapsing and national economic growth became negative as the recession deepened.

Chapter 4

♦

There are vast deposits of natural gas below the surface of the earth trapped in layers of shale rock. Existence of these vast energy reserves has been known for years, the cost of extracting that gas was the issue. Once the price of oil increased to a high enough level, it suddenly became profitable enough to extract gas from layers of shale rock by using drilling methods capable of fracturing the shale to release the gas so it could be withdrawn. A similar situation existed with people just outside of the requirements to qualify for home loans.

The solution to the problem of not being able to extend loans to people who fell below the line was a simple one, move the line. The drill bit was the subprime loan. The water pumped in to fracture the rocks were adjustable rate, one-hundred percent and other mortgage instruments that allowed buyers to acquire homes with low to no initial investment. The key was to create a large enough pool of homebuyers to generate a bubble substantial enough to drill into. You have to remember the collective spending on shelter of this group of people was largely in the form of rental payments. Transforming this enormous revenue stream from rental cash flow to mortgage payments was a critical development.

Once the rules of a long standing game are changed, the players tend to change also. Abuse was destined to rear its ugly head. Why sell a homeowner a home on a conventional mortgage if they would take a subprime loan with a higher payout for the loan officer. Why not move the buyer up to a larger house by using looser subprime credit standards for the new home loan. Redlining was a practice of not providing certain services such as mortgage lending to certain areas based upon who lived there and where it was located. When subprime lending came along, redlining became redefined as going into those same areas and pushing subprime loans with excessive fees even if individual applicants qualified for conventional mortgage terms and rates. Another sizable segment of new home buyers couldn't resist getting a home with an extra bedroom or in-ground pool, so they moved on to a mortgage with a more flexible payment structure. A considerable portion of those individual mistakes in judgment would come back to cause countless sleepless nights in the future.

Once a renter became a homeowner several actions were triggered. New homeowners spent money on furniture, appliances, yard care and powered several segments of the wider economy. The most important change that occurred when a former renter became a homeowner was a mortgage obligation. A mortgage is a financial instrument collateralized by the value of the home it financed and required monthly payments from the homeowner. Imagine the fractured rental rock releasing this huge new pool of subprime mortgage value ready for exploitation. A massive creation of wealth on paper also generated an enormous revenue stream in the form of mortgage payments to banks and mortgage companies.

What was the real impact of this creation of a new class of homeowners? Instability was the primary result. Traditional mortgage rules required homeowners to keep their home mortgage payments generally in the 30 percent range of their total monthly income. Those more liberal subprime home loans allowed mortgage payments over 50 percent and some as high as 60 percent of the homeowner's income. The combination of higher interest rates charged on subprime loans and borrowers with less stable credit profiles created a ticking financial time bomb waiting to explode.

The failure within the subprime lending area upon closer examination represented a huge setback for future financial prospects for millions of people. Think about the burden a foreclosure on a credit report places on someone trying to move forward in life. It would have been better for an individual to delay getting a home instead of what happened with subprime lending. Some of the allowed ratios of home payment to income ratios created an unsustainable financial situation. For many people it would take something a simple as an unexpected automobile repair expense to start them down the road towards foreclosure.

I hear various opinions that what happened with the foreclosure created the greatest loss of wealth in history in certain demographics of our country. There is some truth to the wealth loss when it is looked at from the standpoint of losing a home as an asset component of personal net worth. Another way to view what happened is to consider the acquisition of the homes under unsustainable terms a creation of false wealth. That was my supposition earlier when I mentioned that the subprime boom was of greatest benefit to investors given the ability of Wall Street to exploit the mortgages as tradable securities. Homebuyers had to live with the emotional and financial scars created by the real loss of their homes and credit standing.

Owning a home was once a hard fought prize earned by people who were diligent with their finances. Paying bills on time, using credit carefully and saving for a down payment created the type of discipline that prepared an individual to meet a 30-year obligation of monthly payments. The lowered bar of subprime lending allowed those still financially immature to get in over their heads and caused everybody to suffer later.

The existence of new subprime homeowners was not an inherent problem on its own merit. If a high foreclosure rate among this group took place in a conventional sense, it would be problematic, but not catastrophic. The problem was the huge financial empire built with subprime loans as part of the foundation. Do you remember the mathematical wizards tasked with inventing new mortgage derived financial instruments? A huge bubble was generated on the back of risky subprime mortgages. Mortgage backed securities were fashioned with the inclusion of subprime and A-paper home loans. As mentioned earlier, high-risk loans were combined with low-risk loans and divided into something commonly referred to as a mortgage backed security (MBS), which was like a bond. Another financial instrument called a CDO, which simply means collateralized debt obligation, was a bundle of MBS and created an investment grade vehicle. So what you had was a second level pooled mortgage backed financial instrument built upon a foundation of an original pooled mortgage backed security. The entire structure depended on home mortgage payments. In addition, CDO issues were often pledged as collateral for loans.

CDO vehicles were given risk ratings by trusted debt rating agencies so potential investors could judge if they should buy into the new financial instruments. Once those hybrid debt products received their stamps of approval, the game was on. This was going to be a world wide hustle. Go big or don't go at all. Residential mortgage backed CDO investments were wildly successful. Why would they not sell? The product was secured by real estate and monthly mortgage payments. The most respected debt rating agencies had bestowed their trusted risk ratings and to top it off, the products had a quasi-insurance policy available to buffer any losses. The credit default swap was one more assurance it was safe to invest in this can't lose proposition. When mortgage defaults mounted at the base of this pyramid the whole structure collapsed and brought several investment banks to their knees. Collateralized Debt Obligations were general and all were not comprised of residential mortgage backed securities, it is just in this case where all the problems occurred.

Often it is said, the devil is in the details. Withdrawal was far worse than the high. Foreclosures grew and the revenue stream was interrupted. Credit default swaps had insufficient assets backing them and the ivory towers collapsed under their own weight. The captains of the financial universe were hunkered down in luxurious bunkers bought with bounty gained during the previous period of excess. Some of those chief executive officers, hedge fund managers and investment bankers made hundreds of millions of dollars pushing the envelope with residential mortgage backed CDO trading.

Economic carnage mounted all across the country as enticing subprime home loans exploded in the face of panicked homeowners. Foreclosures grew and the backlash of anger echoed from coast to coast. All too soon the curtain was pulled back exposing the real culprits. The list was long and included the homeowners themselves. This well oiled machine was the nation's new economic engine, but in reality it was a contraption powered by the equivalent of giant rodents furiously running inside circular wheels. This was a global financial Enron. In fact, the similarities were striking with arcane accounting, inflated asset values and corporate malfeasance on a worldwide scale. The Enron comparison ends due to the much broader scale of the latest financial crisis. What Enron did to its stakeholders, the mortgage backed security meltdown did to the entire American economy.

Anytime something of that magnitude explodes and threatens the stability of the country, the first order of business for the real culprits was to affix blame on a less powerful group to divert the public's attention. The first demon was the mortgage broker. Mortgage brokers were accused with a broad brush of trickery, abuse of trust and lack of concern for their victims. Some national figures even characterized mortgage brokers as fly-by-night operators. Although there were enough abuses to go around. Mortgage brokers were not the cause of the subprime loan crisis. Mortgage brokers only acted as agents that offered home-loan products that mortgage companies created. All of the rules and qualification criteria set forth to allow someone to qualify for a mortgage came from lenders. There were some brokers who broke the rules and acted unethically, but individuals with ethical flaws could be found in all professions. Some large mortgage companies were actually fined for abusing applicants with exorbitant fees and other predatory practices. In fact the blame game moved from mortgage brokers to the homeowners themselves. It was only after the economic downturn hit full force and compelled the true culprits to raise their hands because they needed to be rescued from their own folly, then the truth was known.

The dominoes fell fast and hit virtually every sector of the economy. One of the most insidious aspects of the mortgage crisis was how it was able to inflict damage upon people who did not have a mortgage at all. Some homeowners owned their property outright and did not have a conventional or subprime loan. Rising foreclosures and a collapse in home sales served to depress everyone's property values.

Chapter 5

♦

Virga is when rain falls from the sky but does not reach the earth. We have a similar situation with our economic system today. With so many of our finished goods now manufactured in other countries, much of what we spent on products failed to reach the bottom levels of our economy. Just as it was theorized that Virga evaporates before it reaches the ground, money spent on foreign manufactured goods does not evaporate, it simply falls into the economy of another country. That is so crucial when a nation slides into recession today compared to years past?

During most previous economic downturns in the United States the return of consumption by individuals and business fueled prosperity from the retail level down to raw material extraction. That vertical model exists in few instances today. The days of completely single-country-sourced complex products are distant memories.

With modern global economics, manufacturing sources may be scattered around the globe with various components fabricated in different nations or continents. Because of worldwide parts sourcing, there is a diminished effect when the final product is sold to the consumer. Only one entity garners the largest profit margin and it goes to where the company is based. What is different about internationally acquired components that create a sophisticated final product is a global diffusion of profit that traditionally stayed in the United States. I call that economic effect, financial fragmentation.

Worldwide sourcing and manufacturing enabled products to be snapped together like puzzles upon final assembly and it created a similar scattering of revenue and profit. An automobile sold in the United States, but produced in Japan or Europe only left the retailer and distributor profit in America.

As mentioned earlier, we now have foreign automobile assembly operations located in the United States. Most of the components are shipped over as finished parts ready for assembly into the final product. From a practical standpoint, the actual fabrication was still accomplished in another country. My definition of manufacturing is turning raw materials into a finished product.

If the body panels, engine block and other vital parts were manufactured in another nation, that portion of the vertical chain of profit never reached the ground in the United States. I recall participating in an internship at General Motors in Saginaw, Michigan during the late 1970s. Plants manufacturing almost every component of GM vehicles were scattered around the area. There was a malleable plant, which was a massive iron foundry, making a variety of metal parts. Nearby were transmission, gear and various other factories fabricating subassemblies in what was an integrated process largely contained within the borders of a single nation. That system created a revenue flow from retail sales that cascaded down to the iron ore mines.

Why would a foreign company build an assembly plant in the United States? There are only a few reasons. When the cost of importing finished products in sufficient quantities to meet demand exceeds the cost of shipping in individual parts for final assembly in the target market, the decision is simple. Take the example of an automobile. One characteristic of an assembled automobile is bulk. The dead space of an assembled car was required when an individual used it for transportation; however, it reduced the number of vehicles a cargo ship could transport at one time. Now consider if the same car was shipped as unassembled components. A cargo container ship loaded with engines, body panels and other parts could be tightly packed with little wasted space. More unassembled vehicles could occupy the same cargo ship space compared to completed automobiles.

Sure, foreign assembly plant employees earned a decent hourly wage, however the rest of the revenue stream from the sale of the car had changed dramatically. The dealer made a profit when the vehicle was sold. The salesman earned a commission and the dealer's service department made downstream revenue. Transportation of the vehicles from the plant to dealerships was also in the profit picture, but something was missing? That was where the flow of profit became like the rain never reaching the ground. After the retail sale occurred and the bank made a deposit to the dealer's bank account, the money trail took a detour from the United States back across the ocean to the home base of the automobile company. Once the money landed on foreign shores it then began to hit the ground level of the profit chain. If the raw materials, foundry, engine plant and other plants were all located in another country, then the bulk of the profits resided there also. Effectively, profits that powered our economy in the past were now creating wealth in other lands. Multiply this by countless other outsourced or imported products and an environment has been created that makes recovery from an economic downturn extremely difficult.

As mentioned in the prior example of the sales transaction occurring when the car was sold in the United States really dealt with the lowest amount of profit at the retail level. The much greater wholesale profit landed in a foreign bank account. The closed steel mills, auto plants, appliance factories ad infinitum are the headstones marking the death of profit distribution points. The allocation of profit at defunct facilities was in the form of wages, payments to suppliers and subsequent spending of those earnings in the various communities. In other words, a plant closing was like a ship sinking and the vacuum created as it went under pulled down local businesses that existed largely to serve the factory and its employees.

The prior situation applies to foreign headquartered companies. What about companies based in America whose executives decided to ship certain functions to foreign countries or source products completely from firms based in other nations.

In times past the downtown area of local cities and towns were centers of retail commerce and where everybody could be seen on any Saturday. In retailing there was a model of manufacturer, broker, distributor, retailer to consumer. Over the years the largest retailers have transitioned to a model of manufacturer, retailer to consumer. What happened to the broker and distributor? They were replaced by in-house functions of the retailers with buyers, warehousing and transportation departments. Even if manufacturing was separate it was often near captive and so dependent on the retailer that losing their primary client would virtually put the company out of business. Capturing the manufacturer was only step one. Step two was to lower the cost of the product sold in stores which also meant a lower-cost supplier had to be found. Suppliers wanted to retain their large retail customers so they reduced expenses. In cases like this, the most difficult cost to reduce was labor. The easiest way to reduce labor cost was to move production to a location where the normal labor costs were less by default. Once the out-of-country shift to lower-cost labor markets started, it became a race to the floor. Made in the U.S.A. became an increasingly rare label?

A long list developed of industries where manufacturing shifted to lower-cost foreign labor centers and it read like a hit list. Manufacturing of textiles, clothing, appliances, personal computers, televisions and many other products found new homes. Each time an industry left the country, there was a hole left in a community, state or region. The next wave was foreign acquisition of American companies, even the largest domestic beer company is under foreign ownership. Support functions such as customer service call centers were shifted elsewhere with many displaced jobs landing in India. High-speed voice and data transmission on a worldwide scale made location irrelevant for telephone support function. Information-help desks and other tasks performed using high-speed network communications were perfect targets for relocation.

Natural barriers of time, language, distance and oceans had been rendered irrelevant in the modern age. There was a time when products from a foreign country were rare treats and prized for their unique qualities. In today's world it was not so much the unique native creations of less developed nations that had value as much as the sought after economic desperation of a cheap labor force. The real prize had changed. Shifting production from high-cost-labor content in the United States to an ultra-low-cost workforce, in Vietnam for example, allowed labor savings to translate into higher profits for the parent company. The often squalid conditions that foreign workers endured were of little concern because they were faceless production capacity. Safety of the foreign made products only became an issue after the fact whenever a recall would be required after an actual or potential danger to the buying public would surface. We had two instances of product safety issues involving Chinese manufactured products. One episode concerned tainted pet food. The bad pet food resulted in the death of several animals in the United States. Another incident was related to toys that contained dangerous levels of lead that could have placed children in danger. Different standards for safety worldwide tend to create a tenuous environment when it comes to ensuring safety for American consumers. Safety and environmental standards took a back seat to increasing profits.

Company executives received bonuses for increasing profit margins and earnings per share. Displaced American employees often accepted jobs in retail, at much lower pay, selling foreign made products they once produced in this country. New retail associates watched millions in bonuses going to CEOs with the knowledge that the bonuses came from wages formerly earned by themselves and their laid-off factory coworkers. The ability of proud individuals to cope with the loss of commitment from their employers was a testament to the adaptability of the human spirit. What could have resulted in lasting bitterness transformed itself into a drive to do whatever was required to meet ongoing responsibilities.

Everything discussed before was just part of the problem with the economic collapse that emerged near the end of the second term of President George W. Bush. Now it is time for average citizens to reflect and take their share of responsibility for the failure of our economy. We have created a situation where it is more difficult for us to pull ourselves out of a severe economic downturn because so much of what we spend has a greatly diminished impact in our own country.

Chapter 6

♦

Contrary to popular reporting, there were more bubbles bursting than just mortgage, lending and housing. There was a detonation of the overconsumption bubble. Overconsumption is a disease, afflicting many in the industrialized world. How many people really need a new flat-screen television, furniture or automobile every few years? I have a refrigerator that is 20 years old and it still works perfectly. The refrigerator is white and was relegated to the garage 9 years ago because it did not match the black appliances in my new home when we moved in the year 2000. The acquisition of a black refrigerator was a purchase based upon want instead of need. The difference between demand based upon actual need and demand based upon desire was the "false demand" portion of our economy. The problem with false demand is real jobs are dependent upon sustaining that elevated level of consumption. One of the issues we deal with in today's society is a phenomenon I have labeled "complex commodities".

The term "complex commodity" refers to products or services with intricate technology, skill requirement and design, but once conceived, they can be manufactured or replicated in great quantities.

Some examples of complex commodities are printers, computers, televisions, telephone service, air travel, etc. Modern production techniques and open markets have increased the availability of those products and services to the point that some consumers view them like they view different brands of soap. Due to production efficiencies, these items became relatively inexpensive to acquire and commanded increasingly slim profit margins due to excess supply. The world has the capacity to produce many times over the number of computers, televisions and air flights than we can consume on a real need basis.

How many of us bought a new flat-screen HDTV set because we wanted the viewing experience and not because our current set had failed. The same thing can be said of many of the computers, flights and automobiles sold over the last 10 to 15 years. Did we need all of those items to live a fulfilled life, the answer is staring us in the face as consumption died for most discretionary items. Airlines have parked jetliners. High-end electronics are sold in every conceivable outlet from home theatre specialty stores to big-box warehouse discounters. Automobile manufacturers practically use dealer lots as storage facilities for vast amounts of unsold inventory.

When our economy went on a downward slide it became evident that much of our consumer spending was of a frivolous nature. With the prospect of potential job losses, home foreclosures and shrinking retirement portfolios, discretionary consumer spending all but ceased. We had been living in an environment with a negative savings rate fueled by cashing in home equity, easy credit terms and an insatiable appetite for the latest in electronic entertainment. With the consumer demand spending spigot turned off, the corporate casualties were quick to appear. Circuit City, an erstwhile nationwide retailer of electronics, ceased to exist. Circuit City followed nationwide companies Linens and Things and Sharper Image to the grave. These companies had one thing in common; they sold products people could live without. The overconsumption bubble had burst and in one fell swoop, people returned to the basics of life. Now the clock ticks as time wears on with the negative momentum of the economy building upon itself like an avalanche rolling down a mountain sweeping away everything in its path. Legendary business brands such as General Motors and Chrysler were near walking corpses kept alive by government ventilators pumping life sustaining currency into their systems.

Even fabled moguls of business had started to crack under the pressure of their declining investment portfolios. A share of stock of many legendary firms could be acquired for less than the price of a premium cup of coffee. The screams of "Fix the banks and everything else be damned", emanated from those embroiled in the value of stocks, bonds and trust funds. This is where the cultural divide lives. Business tycoons appeared on cable television shows with shrill protestations and proclamations of doom. Even among billionaires, their ability to deliver calm economic analysis ended when some of their massive walls of personal wealth began to crumble.

"Screw those people out there huddled in their tract homes trying to hang on in the face of economic turmoil. Get the stock market back up. To hell with healthcare reform, get the jagged stock trend line going northward again. Forget extending unemployment benefits, who cares, have you seen my trust fund performance? Spend the money by sucking all of those toxic assets out of the banks so we can get our credit going," was the lament of moguls far and wide.

Had anything changed at all? Now the general public was robbed again by bailing out the same institutions that destroyed the economy by literally gambling with mortgage back debt instruments. Now adding insult to injury, taxpayers were asked to be a toxic asset sewage treatment plant for the worthless remains of rampant financial irresponsibility of banks and investment firms. The picture paints itself as the only thing trickling down was the same thing that had fallen on the heads of the average taxpayers for years, waste matter.

Business tycoons told President Obama to focus on the economy and put everything else on the back burner. The President had a different idea, let me give you an example. The house you have lived in for twenty-five years was destroyed in a storm. One builder recommends for you to rebuild it to the same specifications as twenty-five years ago. A different builder advises you to take advantage of this great opportunity to change everything and prepare for the future. Renewable-energy technology is available, network cabling can be incorporated and more durable building materials can be used in the construction. Which would you do? We were going to go through this recession regardless of what kind of plans that were put in place. The issue was how we came out of this downturn. Will we be the same country with the same vulnerabilities as before? Will we still be dependent on foreign energy in the form of petroleum? Will our companies still compete with an additional burden of healthcare costs on their backs when their foreign based competition have national health care systems in their home countries? Do we emerge with the same inadequate education system? The issue is not will we go through this recession, but how we come out.

If we came out of this downturn a different country with a new clean energy system, with vehicles using little to no petroleum and in-country sourced energy supplies, then the United States would be resurrected anew. Resurrection means we would be in control of our own financial destiny and not subject to outside forces in critical areas such as energy prices and supply manipulation. On the other hand, if we came out of this financial downturn with the country's economy structured in the same way it was before, we would just be waiting for the next energy, healthcare or trade crisis to bring us down again.

If we fail to put a healthcare plan in place that covers everyone in this country that is not tied to employment, then our government has failed us in a major way. Given the rate of job loss right now we have millions more men, women and children who are not covered by health insurance in case of illness. The point is not simply free health care but a safety net for those unable to fend for themselves such as children,

What will we do, rebuild the country using an obsolete blueprint or turn the page and create an economy suited for the current century we live in?

Chapter 7

♦

We have seen the ravages of overconsumption, easy credit and how it has negative effects on the economy and individuals. Given how long Americans have lived this way, it is hard to envision how life was before all of this came about.

I recall a time when I perceived credit cards as something used by business people for travel and other purposes where cash was impractical. My parents never used credit cards and the first general credit card I used was company issued for business expenses.

So what did people do before the mass issuance of plastic charge cards to almost every breathing human?

Sometimes inspiration comes in the strangest places. While I was eating lunch at a McDonald's, I overhead a conversation that crystallized the point of this segment. I assumed it was a mother and daughter sitting behind me.

One of the women was distraught about how none of the major department stores offered lay-a-way plans.

"We need that," she said.

I had a flashback to how my mother purchased most of my school clothes every year. We would go to the department store downtown and I would select the pants, shirts and shoes I wanted to wear to school the next year. I normally would get clothes from a long-departed regional store named J. B. White. After gathering up my preferred items, we would take them upstairs to the lay-a-way department.

By paying a small fee to set the goods aside, the clerk would start a ticket with the purchase price divided into a series of periodic payments. If for some reason a customer could not make one of their scheduled payments, they could remit a fee to extend the hold on the goods and make up the missed payment later. Upon making the last payment, the merchandise would be handed over to my mother and I had new clothes to wear to school. This was a normal way of doing business during the 1960s. The main characteristic of lay-a-way plans was the lack of residual debt when the products were turned over to the customer. The second unique thing about that pay-as-you-go system was the personal relationship created between customer and merchant. The third and most critical aspect of that seemingly simple way of doing business was the automatic manner of how it forced people to live within their budget constraints.

A seemingly simple lament at lunch echoed a sense of simmering frustration that many are living with who feel they do not matter in the modern America equation. Existing on the fringes of society has become a way of life for many in the country. I have to wonder how so many people have almost faded into societal invisibility in many ways. It seems that regular citizens are valued for votes and buying power. Every holiday shopping season and election cycle the average citizen becomes the most important people in the country. After their periodic value expires, the attention goes back to the noteworthy and occasional celebrity who rises from the masses via some contrived reality show. The rest of us return to our status as inhabitants of flyover and drive-by locales. Because having the price of is the way the game is played today, those that cannot afford a ticket get to watch through the window. The women at lunch were expressing their displeasure of being forced to look through the window.

The loss of pay-as-you-go in the form of plans such as lay-a-way or a local merchant opening up an account was caused by the disappearance of many locally owned businesses. Credit cards replaced local store credit accounts, but also opened up the floodgates of debt accumulation. Lay-a-way and similar arrangements forced people to live within their means, but credit cards created a false sense of wealth.

Credit cards have also placed borrowers in the position to be squeezed by interest rate increases that go up to 30 percent or more. Credit card debt is an insidious trap that has ensnared millions. Banks are brazen enough to survive with the help of billions of dollars in taxpayers' money while choking the life out of their lifeline with rate increases. Sharp increases in credit card balance interest rates do the same thing to card users that a python does to its victim. A python squeezes its prey in a way that does not allow the trapped animal to inhale whenever it allows air to escape from its lung. The rate increases on credit card balances may raise periodic payments to such an extent that they could slowly drag someone under as their ability to pay the higher amounts decreases ever month. The 0 percent introduction rate was the bait, but the sharp interest rate increase is the hook and it hurts.

A shark tank existed below the credit cards ranks and many were being devoured by pay-day, income-tax advance and pawn-shop loans. Rent-to-own stores were also waiting for people who could not live in the world of credit cards. Unfortunately there were more citizens headed for the feeding frenzy because the wreckage left by the foreclosure crisis was sending people to the bottom rungs of the credit rating ladder.

Chapter 8

_____

♦

I am sure most people have heard the term, too big to fail, when it comes to certain companies. AIG, Citigroup and General Motors all fell into the category of too big to fail. Exactly what does being too big to fail mean?

A company is deemed to be too big to fail when the resulting negative economic and social fallout from its failure is unacceptably damaging to the nation.

I take the reverse view and say many of those organizations are too big to exist. To understand what I mean, we need to go back in time before massive business consolidation created some of the modern day corporate behemoths. I will use a local bank as a simple example. When I moved from a rural area to Dallas in the early 1980s there was an institution named Gibraltar Savings and Loan. Through multiple mergers it changed from

75

Gibraltar Savings and Loan to First Texas Savings, Bank of America (California) and now Bank of America (Nationsbank- North Carolina).

There was a time that I made sure I went to my bank and withdrew money if I was going to visit my hometown about three hours east of Dallas. There were not any branches of my bank in east Texas. Currently, I have flown to New Jersey, Chicago, Phoenix, California and Hawaii with the ability to withdraw money from automatic teller machines owned by my bank in each state. Mergers and acquisitions in banking were but one example of countless combinations of companies that created these massive institutions. This was not a phenomenon limited to banking but occurred in other industries as well. Some institutions grew organically to nationwide and worldwide status through the sheer success of their business models. Wal-Mart is the perfect example of a company that started small and expanded under its own steam.

If you identify who is too big to fail, you, by default, have identified those firms that are too big to exist. Why are they too big to exist, that all depends on the rules they operate under. The lack of regulatory oversight that led to the economic meltdown that emerged in the fall of 2008 created a large list of organizations too big to exist. Some firms are too big to exist because of the multiplier effect of their actions on the economy and society at large.

The first category of companies most individuals could view as too big to exist would be financial institutions that became intertwined in multiple segments of the economy. When consumer deposits, investment banking, mortgage lending and commercial lending all come from one nationwide institution, the effect of a failure is too broad. The decision multiplier effect of a nationwide financial institution affects millions of people in one fell swoop. A decision to raise credit card interest rates adversely affects the budgets and buying power of a vast amount of people in a way a local or regional bank cannot, given the size of their client base. A local bank might be more hesitant to make drastic moves such as credit card interest rate changes out of concern for losing customers to a competitive institution. Massive institutions with millions of account holders may calculate that the increase in interest revenue will outstrip any marginal customer losses. The barriers for customers to move their business to another institution might be much higher as some clients have credit cards, mortgages, retirement accounts and investment accounts with the same bank. Smaller financial companies may not have the same range of services as a large bank and would be more prone to losing customers. As we can see clearly by the latest problems created when large financial firms encountered solvency problems, they can bring down many other businesses with them. Even if a large bank failure would not cause other institutions to go under, the sheer size of their customer base could trigger a large run on the bank as well as create a confidence issue for customers of other institutions. Local and regional institutions have a limited impact by their very nature in the event of failure. Local and regional banks fail with scant notice from a nationwide news standpoint except for a brief mention if there is any acknowledgement at all.

What about other large institutions outside of the financial industry? What if a large retailer fails? We have an example in Circuit City. Circuit City went under without a whimper from anyone about bailing them out with government assistance. There were 30,000 jobs lost, yet no outcry. The public simply lined up to take advantage of the bargains. There was not a larger impact on the economy, national security or other vital national interests which determines how the government views business failures. The next day after the last Circuit City store closed, their former customers could simply shop at Best Buy, Wal-Mart or any number of retailers selling similar products. Sure those thirty thousand employees are now with the legion of people seeking jobs or drawing unemployment benefits, but it was viewed as an isolated event. There is a long history of large retail failures without the government lifting a financial finger to help. Do you remember these names Montgomery Ward, KB Toys and Service Merchandise? Some of these legendary names still exist as the brand was sold to other companies who use them, but the original companies are gone. The moral of this story is that retailers are considered expendable. Now if Wal-Mart was on the verge of failure we would see if the expendable retailer rule would apply with the company employing over two million people.

Why don't we just allow the automakers to go under? Large retailers, airlines and in the distant past, automobile manufacturers, were allowed to fail, then why not now? Well now times have changed. It is hard for people today to realize a time existed when there were more American automobile companies than we have today. Studebaker, Packard and American Motors have all gone to the corporate wrecking yard in the sky. In the early days of automobiles there were many who felt they could do it better than anyone else. It took years for the industry to shake itself down to a few competitors. The survivors in this capital and labor intensive business finally whittled itself down to three dominant players in the United States. General Motors, Ford and Chrysler are the remaining major players of the United States based automobile manufacturers. Chrysler in fact has been near failure before and survived with government assistance. Chrysler was later purchased by the Germany based manufacturer of Mercedes-Benz vehicles and is now a unit of a private investment company.

In general, the too big to fail tag is placed on large companies in certain industries the government considers vital to the continued functioning of the country. Petroleum, air travel, finance and automobile manufacturing are the primary sectors where the largest companies in those industries might be deemed too vital to go out of business abruptly.

Let us walk back in time to the days when I was in high school during the mid 1970s, a time when foreign cars were truly foreign. Except for the Volkswagen Beetle and Van, every other foreign car seemed like it came from another planet. Nissan was then called Datsun and I don't recall laying eyes on a Toyota. Japanese cars were considered cheap, strange and hard to repair. One of my neighbors owned a red Datsun B210 which we derided at every opportunity. There was nothing I enjoyed better than blowing a Datsun or Volkswagen off the road with my V-8 engine equipped Chevrolet Impala. Fast forward to the present and things have changed dramatically. In 2008 the best selling automobile in the country was the Toyota

Camry. Toyota cars regularly win NASCAR races even though they started competing in the top level of the series in 2007. Assembly plants of foreign owned automobile companies now exist on United States soil. This is truly a different world.

To understand why the desire to save American automobile manufacturers is so strong is more than a simple question with one answer. Sure the ability to maintain heavy manufacturing in the country is vital as we saw during World War II. In times of potential national security crisis our country would be vulnerable with dependence on other countries for military vehicles. The ability to switch plants from consumer to military vehicle production would be severely limited. The worst case scenario would be for hostilities to ensue between the headquarters country of our automobile suppliers and the United States. Can you imagine an embargo on vehicle shipments and production against the country due to some international disagreement?

As the future of the United States automobile companies hangs in the balance, it may be time to look at the three companies separately. Are all of the companies in the same relative position in the marketplace? The answer to that question is a resounding no. Of the three companies it seems Chrysler was the most expendable. Chrysler had the weakest product line and was far behind in creating advanced technology for alternative fuel vehicles. General Motors was a stalwart and seemed to be the focus of most of the government's efforts at rescue. GM had a promising vehicle for alternative fuel transportation in the Chevy Volt. The primary issue with a potential failure of GM would be the massive unemployment and damage to a supply chain that served many other automobile companies. GM had the distinction of having its CEO dismissed by the President of the United States. Ford had managed to move forward without government assistance as they secured a massive amount of private financing before credit markets froze.

There are more complex issues at play. Many won't tell you how keeping automobile manufacturing owned by United States firms is the key to future self-determination in the area of energy independence. If we had no United States based automobile companies, the ability of the nation to move to new alternative-energy-fuel based vehicles that would free the country from dependence on foreign fuel sources is blocked. Imagine Toyota, Nissan and other foreign automakers as the only suppliers of vehicles to the country. How much influence do we have to move companies based in other countries to migrate to new clean-energy sources. Even if the vehicles shifted to fuel cell or battery power, we will have traded dependence on one foreign energy source for another. Without the ability to control the new vehicle fuel technology, we would be subject to the fluctuations in prices of new energy sources as inevitable shortages and price spikes would occur. The United States without a home-grown automobile industry is frankly a place I would not recognize. "See the USA in a Toyota" does not have the right ring to it.

The most compelling reason to maintain automobile manufacturing ownership in this country is once it is gone, it will not return.

Chapter 9

♦

Just as a Hurricane in nature will flush out hidden rats, roaches and snakes of all types, a financial storm will flush out human serpents, liars and cheats. These financial sociopaths are hard to identify in the midst of prosperity. They walk among us dressed in the finest business attire. During times of plenty these predators are difficult to detect as they blend in with the rest of society. Often the worst of the vermin are held in the highest of esteem due to the positions of authority they occupy.

A reptile of Anaconda proportions emerged after the financial winds began to howl. Bernard Madoff was turned in by his own offspring. Cloaked in the ultimate of respectability, Madoff left a $64 billion high mountain of financial wreckage. Incredibly this was someone who owned the legitimacy mantle. As former chairman of the NASDAQ stock exchange, no one would suspect Bernard Madoff of purposely perpetrating the largest investment fraud in United States history by a single individual. The net was cast wide by Bernard as he bilked retirees, athletes, movie stars and pension funds. None were safe from the carnage as people instantly went from perceived financial security to living on food stamps. People with plans for retirement suddenly had nightmare thoughts of working until at death's door. There should be a special place reserved in the hottest corner of hell for Bernard Madoff, the king of scammers.

Madoff Investment Securities was started in 1960, allegedly the false investment scheme began in 1990. Any company in the securities business has to file reports and is subject to reviews from the Securities and Exchange Commission. The nature of the reality is so unbelievable, I would not dare write it as a piece of fiction because it would not be viewed as credible. The very idea that for almost two decades, if that was the case, a massive string of investors were kept in a state of euphoria by investment payouts from other people pulled into the scheme. In effect Bernard Madoff was operating what some refer to as a Ponzi scheme, which is to pay old investors with money from current or new investors. The scheme Madoff constructed was massive and stretched around the globe.

Since Madoff was the largest serpent that came out, other lesser but no less despicable vipers slitered into the sunlight.

There was an $8-billion rip-off here and a $50-million scam there, with countless others to unfold as time moved on. These perpetrators were not standing on street corners dealing drugs or snatching purses in parking lots, but did far worse. This class of criminal used the trappings of legitimacy to entice people to willingly entrust them with their hard earned treasure. These charlatans had the most valuable thing someone intent upon practicing fraud on a massive scale could obtain, the confidence of their intended victims. This was the very definition of the confidence game, which is more commonly known as the con game. I do not intent to allow these criminals to parade around as symbols of propriety simply because they look a certain way, wear expensive business clothes and live in luxury accommodations. These were not the captains of commerce; on the contrary, these people were base criminals who operated in a highly sociopathic manner. Their destruction was not perpetrated with guns, drugs or prostitution but with something much harder to read, a firm handshake and warm smile.

First Timothy 6:10 of the New International Bible states, "For the love of **money** is a root of all kinds of **evil**. Some people, eager for **money**, have wandered from the faith and pierced themselves with many griefs."

The question is who was the above passage meant to admonish? Of course those with ill intent cannot escape their role in this episode of financial debauchery. Victims who were drawn into those scams have to grudgingly search their souls for their motives that ultimately led to their financial demise. Salmon swim upstream to spawn, most other things in nature flow with the prevailing currents. Was it logical to believe in magic and magicians? Supermen able to create double digit returns regardless of the prevailing direction of the overall economy were too much for some to resist. How did these financial genies practice their magic in order to know what investment moves to make even when the economy went into decline. Many threw their financial future into the hands of theses apparent geniuses and now we know the truth. I loathe these heartless humans who can destroy the present and future of thousands of people without apparent remorse, yet the warning siren of the tritest of advice sounds loudly. We all know about things that appear too good to be true, now we have another glaring example of how painful and real that phrase can be.

Madoff and his ilk fall into the category of pure thievery by brazen individuals. The financial institutions that plunged the United States economy into a freefall with a tether line attached to the rest of the world, lawfully gambled with the collective wealth of millions without their knowledge. Madoff was led off in handcuffs, yet many others have thus far escaped the perpetrator walk of shame.

What did these people know and when did they know it? How long were traders manipulating the system to delay the inevitable crash so they could cash out at full value before the rest of the oblivious passive investors were wiped out by plunging stock values? John and Jane Q. Public with their retirement funds invested in the stock market were hit with a financial sledgehammer as experts shrugged in bewilderment. Endless talking heads screamed and shouted "How could this happen?" as panic set in. George W. Bush, the 43rd President of the United States, would step up behind microphones, when he could be found, with a deer-in the-headlights expression and issue dire statements. John McCain, one of the candidates to be the 44th President, went off course in an erratic pattern committing to solve the financial crisis. A third man competing to be President, at the least, behaved rationally. That consistent behavior, in large part, gained Barack Obama the election victory for President.

Some have likened this recession to an economic 9-11. Others see it as a financial Hurricane. Neither of those comparisons hold muster. Outside forces attacked us when 9-11 occurred. A hurricane is an unpredictable and destructive phenomenon of nature. The economic collapse of 2008 was not from outside forces, but was self-inflicted. While the impacts of what took place as our economy declined were destructive, it was far from natural and in hindsight should not only have been predictable, but expected.

The cries from inside the very firms that collapsed, expressing how perplexed they were at the failure of their collateralized debt obligation business, stretched the limits of credulity. The greater question was how creators of a business model could be unaware of the continued erosion in that sector. The sign of something being afoot was the figurative bursting of the dam as all of the carnage seemed to spring forward through multiple breaches at once. Since the problems emerged, the government has been stuffing hundreds of billions of dollars into the holes in attempts to stem the flooding that threatens to sweep everything away lying downstream financially.

There were other mischief makers afoot, but they managed to hide behind veils of the legality of their actions.

Chapter 10

♦

So what happened to the banks and why was credit frozen? Most people heard a constant drumbeat to please fix the banks. As all of the histrionics were taking place, many people wondered how the banks became broken to begin with.

The interesting thing is banks should have never been in this position. Remember commercial banks were institutions that wrote mortgages and held the notes to term in the early days of home loans. The regulatory walls were torn down between commercial banks and investment banks by the repeal of the Glass-Steagall act in 1999. The Glass-Steagall Act created a separation between commercial banks and investment banks in order to prevent conflicts of interest and mitigate risk. With the barriers removed there was nothing to prevent a commercial bank from forming divisions to actively participate in the investment arena.

All of the conditions were set for an incredible creation of wealth, if you measure wealth in money instead of tangible assets. Think about the temptation to cross pollinate inside a large bank holding billions in deposits, home mortgages and investment portfolios. The enticement to leverage separate businesses to assist the growth of the other could not be denied. In general, banks were steamrolled by the real effects of the mortgage crisis.

When home foreclosures began to rise, the homes that formed a substantial portion of the banks asset base began to lose value. As more homes went into foreclosure and the mortgages attached to them became non-performing, the property became the asset of the bank. Those assets were rapidly shrinking because property values were falling. Add mortgage backed securities held by banks as part of it investment portfolio into their asset mix and the credit crisis began. Banks are required to maintain certain asset to loan ratios. As asset values declined the ability of banks to make new loans became more and more restricted. In truth, all lending did not cease, but the standards for loan qualification were much more stringent. What was formerly considered good credit suddenly fell short of the tightened standards for a new loan. The credit market became risk adverse.

Let me give you an example that occurred in the industry where I practice my craft, business equipment sales. Ninety-nine percent of the business I transact requires the customer to obtain lease financing. A customer felt that it was in his best interest to add more capacity to his operation. I was able to obtain an approval for this transaction in August of 2008 within a few seconds on the telephone. Due to an administrative snafu the final processing of the paperwork was delayed and the credit approval expired. During the middle of October 2008, the same leasing company could not get the deal approved again. Three financing companies turned the application down but I was finally able to place the loan with a fourth organization that reviewed the credit application. Since September of 2008, two major leasing companies had exited the office equipment leasing segment of the business.

You have heard about toxic assets clogging the banking system and blocking their ability to lend. Some wanted the government to create a bad bank to clean up the balance sheets of the banks so lending could resume. Just what were reporters talking about on cable news talk shows?

The problem was an unknown amount of mortgage backed assets were sitting on the books of banks and no one wanted to touch them because they had no set value. Billions of dollars of mortgage backed securities were sold worldwide. Due to the home foreclosure crisis, MBS instruments were now worth only a fraction of their face value, but were still held by banks and investment firms as assets. Those devalued and unsalable assets had torpedoed the ability of lending institutions to make new loans. Other actions had also taken place due to the current squeeze. Individuals and companies found their credit accounts reduced or closed altogether. The credit lines businesses relied on for everything from financing inventory to payroll were becoming harder to renew and had caused some companies to shut down.

Conditions in our banking system were very hard to pin down by normal standards. Some small banks were apparently too small to matter and were allowed to fail without much fanfare. Several large banks were being propped up by infusions of government capital while others that behaved more prudently were doing relatively well. One problem affecting all banks was the widening nature of foreclosures as some began to lose their homes because of prolonged unemployment instead of mortgage adjustments. The home asset base continued to decline in value and began to affect banks that were conservative in their lending practices. When the foreclosure crisis would peak was unknown and probably would be determined in hindsight through analyzing historical data. A perfect example of this was the determination of how long the United States had been in a recession before it was declared, which was about one year.

Concrete information was one of the missing pieces of the puzzle because the trading of mortgage backed debt instruments were largely unregulated and unreported. There was not a central clearing house that tracked how many MBS products were sold and resold. Much of this debt went to foreign based buyers and expanded the reach of the negative consequences of home foreclosures in America.

It is clear that companies and countries can no longer make decisions based upon the premise that the effects are strictly localized. We can take the example of competition in various sectors that worldwide markets are here to stay. An example of how an United States based companies have to plan for competition is Boeing considering Airbus. Another case is Caterpillar tractor and its Japanese competitor Komatsu. One final example is Harley-Davidson motorcycles and its foreign competitors.

There can be no denial of how integrated the world economy had become and how it could never be untangled. Obviously having an interconnected world economy has both positive and negative ramifications. Financial turmoil formerly confined to a single nation can now rattle economies many time zones away. In many ways the effect was not unlike an interconnected power grid. It may be time to erect international buffers to cushion the rolling blackout effects of financial downturns from one country to another.

Chapter 11

♦

If this all about banks, why has the insurance company American International Group, better known as AIG, received more money than any other company to prop it up due to the economic downturn? I stopped counting when the figure reached $180 billion. In the face of this staggering amount of assistance to shore up a public corporation came the news of a total of $165 million dollars of bonuses for AIG executives who traded derivatives. The question is what are derivatives?

Upon first blush, it seemed whatever these people traded was derived from something else. Much of it was a form of quasi-insurance policy sold in case the mortgage back obligations investors purchased went into default. Houston, we have a problem.

Remember these words, Credit Default Swap (CDS). Credit Default Swap is what the product was called that investors purchased to protect them in case the mortgage backed securities that they acquired failed. Imagine you are at a blackjack table and the dealer shows an ace and asks if everyone wants insurance against the house hitting a twenty-one. The players are all in heavily with their chip stacks and everybody says they want insurance. The dealer turns over a queen and hits twenty-one, there is only one problem; the dealer does not have enough chips to pay the insurance bets. The dealer only has a fraction of the chips needed and the players are not happy. It comes to light that this dealer was not only taking insurance bets for his table, but for blackjack tables in casinos around the world. The dealer's phone starts to ring with calls from other blackjack tables wanting to pay off their insurance bets. The rest of the casino is operating well, but the insurance bets from the dealer's blackjack table are so large they may bring the entire operation down in order to make the players whole. The prior scenario is what happened to AIG, which is primarily an insurance company with policies insuring individuals and businesses worldwide. AIG is woven into the fabric of businesses to the point that their demise could trigger a cascade of failures worldwide.

AIG has offices and companies worldwide and is involved in everything from automobile insurance to aircraft leasing. One part of the company develops commercial real estate around the globe while another subsidiary does home mortgage lending. In fact AIG owned a subprime mortgage lending company, but closed it as the market for higher risk home loans began to collapse. As you can see, this company is waist deep into the machinery of the world economy. For the most part AIG was a healthy company, except for the division that issued mortgage derivatives to insure investors in Collateralized Debt Obligations against losses. AIG's derivative division became the tail that wagged the dog and still could bring this entire behemoth to the ground. To place things in context, AIG had almost 120,000 employees; the division dealing with Credit Default Swaps had about 450 employees. So it was possible for the activities of less than one quarter of one percent of the firm's employees to wreck the company when its business failed.

To place things into proper perspective, ExxonMobil reported a record annual profit for a United States company of $45.2 billion dollars for the year of 2008. AIG reported the largest quarterly loss in the nation's history for the fourth quarter of 2008 of $61.7 billion dollars. Think about the magnitude of a three-month loss surpassing the annual profit of the world's largest publicly traded company.

The complete failure of AIG was deemed to be a systemic risk to the world economy. As a result of the federal infusion of these billions of dollars, the United States government owns an 80 percent stake in AIG. Now we have to see if our insurance company can climb out of the hole it helped dig the country into.

Chapter 12

♦

It seems class warfare was declared some time ago in various corporate boardrooms and no one informed the blue-collar rank and file workers who actually build things in this country. Think about the difference in attitude and treatment of the American automobile workforce versus Wall Street executives. If you labored on a factory floor for an American automobile company instead of a Wall Street trading floor for an investment firm, then to hell with you. The "to hell with you message" was coming from elected government officials who seemed to be representing companies from foreign countries. The shortsightedness of this approach was stunning. As mentioned earlier in this book, maintaining a significant manufacturing capability is vital to the national security of this country. The only thing apparently vital to the mostly southern lawmakers, whose states had foreign vehicle assembly plants on their soil, was getting re-elected.

The mass psychology of this episode was exposed. Factory workers who represented the one time backbone of the American middle class were portrayed as low-skilled individuals with pay far above what they deserved. How did blue-collar workers become the villains? It was a brilliant piece of spin selling. First spread an outrageous piece of misinformation about the hourly earnings of the automobile worker being over $70 per hour. The second piece was to build up anger against a boogeyman, the United Auto Workers Union. The third and final component was to whip up public anger against the tone-deaf automobile executives who flew into Washington D C on three separate corporate jets. There was almost a demand for the executives of the General Motors and Chrysler to grovel for their government loans while billions were shoveled into the furnaces of banks and financial companies. When did creating real wealth by building tangible products become beneath contempt.

General Motors, Ford Motor Company and Chrysler were suffering from a double dose of trouble. The fear of potential car buyers regarding the economy dried up demand and unit sales dropped. Combine the drop in demand with the higher difficulty of those seeking to buy vehicles in obtaining vehicle loans and it was easy to see the severity of the problem for American automobile manufacturers.

Near the end of April 2009, General Motors announced that it would go into a self-induced coma and shut down 13 assembly plants for up to 11 weeks during the summer of 2009. The purpose of that massive shutdown was to allow inventory levels of vehicles to sell down to manageable levels. In other words, their pipeline was full and it didn't make economic sense to build additional finished product. There will be a ripple effect as some already weak automobile industry suppliers may not survive the temporary loss of business.

One result of GM's cutbacks was the decision to send the 73-year-old car brand Pontiac to join Oldsmobile as a relic of their corporate past. Even with steep cutbacks, GM was not able to avoid going into bankruptcy and filed on June 1, 2009.

Chrysler went into chapter 11 bankruptcy on May 30, 2009, and agreed to sell its assets to Italian automaker Fiat. There was strong opposition from various stakeholders to the sale and whether it would go to completion was in question.

Now let us delve into the realm of burning down your own neighborhood during a riot. Distant history was used to frame the modern United States big three automakers as out of touch companies making low quality products. Vehicles built in the 1970s and early 1980s were used as examples of the current quality coming out of Michigan based automobile companies. Ghosts of the Ford Pinto, Chevy Vega and others were drudged up to recall the bad old days of shoddy automotive quality. The truth is many modern American cars have high levels of quality comparable to foreign made products. Another distortion was to peg the big-three as focusing primarily on fuel-thirsty sports utility vehicles and pickup trucks. What was curiously omitted were the facts about Toyota and Nissan having robust truck and SUV product lines. Both recently plunged headlong into the full-sized pickup truck business. You should not blindly buy into the idea that foreign-made automobiles are automatically superior to American made products. Do your research, take test drives and make your own determination.

Blue collar and service workers in all sectors of the economy took body blows. People creating real worth by taking raw materials and turning them into products others purchased took hits. Service employees in retail, restaurants and other service related fields were also squeezed as discretionary spending dried up.

It was difficult to determine who would survive longer, the retailer whose business had declined or the supplier of the products they sold when restocking orders slowed. It was not easy to conclude because each situation depended upon the financial reserves and strength of each organization.

Ironically one industry at the foundation of the boom became one of the early casualties. New home construction was one of the booming businesses when subprime lending was at its peak. Tract homebuilders converted desserts, fields and beachfronts into Mecca's for eager homebuyers and speculators. When the crash occurred, hammers fell silent and construction workers went from being essential to superfluous in one fell swoop. Failing home builders received token news coverage in the midst of bailout headlines dominating the news cycle on a daily basis. Ironically the house is the real asset at the root of the financial crisis. Many of those newly constructed homes were sold with flexible mortgage financing as an enticement. Many homebuilders had an in-house mortgage company they used as leverage to sell the home. Often if a buyer did not use the builder's captive mortgage company, the free home amenities upgrades were unavailable. Of course the free upgrades were built into the price of the home or interest rate of the loan.

Americans fell in love with money-for-nothing as a career choice and that was at the root of theses problems. We have even managed to create a class of celebrities who are famous for being famous. You know, the romance of day trading stocks, the thrill of flipping houses for quick profits and cashing in on rising home values. We had cable television shows called Flip This House and another titled Flip That House. It seemed more than just the houses had flipped. The mantel of "greed is good" was secretly a point of pride. Individuals who decided not to pursue the quickest path to accumulating money were seen as backwards and risk averse. This time of financial folly caused the country and individuals to amass vast amounts of debt. The veneer of our good life began to be stripped away by the blows reigned upon the populace by the relentless assault of the financial collapse. There was one certainty and it was things would probably never be the same as we attempted to crawl back to a stable financial footing.

Monthly employment loss reports with figures of over 500,000 and 600,000 became a recurring reality. The idea that month after month the country was losing enough jobs to equal the population of cities like Denver, Boston and Seattle was stunning. Continual job losses can cause a recession to morph into a depression. Witnessing bedrock institutions closing, downsizing or taking defensive action shocked the sensibilities of some citizens. It was not difficult to understand people and organizations that decided to adopt a bunker mentality to ride out what they perceive to be a rough economic storm ahead. Sadly these very actions were self-perpetuating and led to downward-rolling snowball as spending on all but the essentials was sharply curtailed.

Chapter 13

♦

On April 3rd 2009 the United States Labor Department reported the unemployment rate had jumped to 8.5 percent after another 663,000 positions were lost in the month of March of the same year. Admittedly, the numbers was high.

Another report by the Associated Press on April 3rd of 2009 stated, since the recession officially started in December of 2007, 5.1 million people had lost their jobs. By adding in part-time workers and discouraged job-seekers the adjusted unemployment rate would have been 15.6 percent in March of 2009.

The previous numbers were alarming, but they still failed to tell the whole story. The real story was in which jobs were lost versus the positions retained by individuals who were still working.

On balance we were trading out higher paying positions in construction and manufacturing for lower wage service positions. Auto-industry employees, carpenters and heavy-equipment operators had joined the unemployment lines. Remember who was doing well in this slowdown, discount stores.

We could not power an economy by losing $20-plus-per-hour jobs and keeping $8-per-hour positions. There would be a point where there were not enough people with purchasing power to keep the $8-per-hour workers employed. Retail and service industry jobs were not immune to elimination. Several national retailers and restaurant chains ceased operations altogether or closed unprofitable locations. Across the country, local service oriented companies had quietly gone out of business.

How were small business owners counted when they decided the time had come to close down their operations. Most entrepreneurs were not eligible for unemployment benefits and therefore were not included in the jobless numbers.

There was one class of unemployed missing from the jobless categories. College graduates finding there were no positions available for them to fill seemed to fall though the classification cracks. Where did out-of-work new graduates go? Many new graduates ended up back at home with their parents. I called this log jam of educated, employable and eager people who found long lines of experienced professionals ahead of them at career fairs, outsource outcasts.

The reason I used the term outsource outcasts because jobs that should be waiting on these enthusiastic college graduates had been sent elsewhere. The loss of manufacturing in the country also took with it positions for engineers, designers and other high-technology based professions. With the economy in a slump, the availability of entry-level professional positions for new college graduates narrowed. Professional positions in sales, accounting and human resources came under pressure when companies were downsizing.

Major companies with manufacturing located in the United States also had regional facilities located across the country. Regional facilities required many of the same functions in accounting, management and human resources as a corporate headquarters. When manufacturing is sent elsewhere, those regional jobs requiring college graduates went away and left a void in the potential career market.

The longer term question was how long would it take before the backlog of job seekers declined enough for recent college graduates to start moving into the workforce in larger numbers. Many found themselves working in positions far below their potential in customer service jobs such as call center representatives. The irony of this was a resetting of the requirements for positions formerly requiring high school diplomas to suddenly stipulate four-year college degrees. The reason the requirements changed was due to an oversupply of available college graduates instead of actual job complexity.

I'm sure most of those college graduates were not planning on careers as $14–per-hour telephone call center representatives. Unfortunately many firms were not in expansion mode. Some companies made a decision to protect the base of business they had instead of investing to gain costly new customers with meant little new hiring.

Chapter 14

♦

Now we come to the dignity gap. What I mean by the dignity gap are the actions Americans were force to take in order to pay their bills.

Older citizens who thought they would be enjoying their golden years have discovered they had fools' gold instead of 24k. Images of people in their seventies trying to re-enter the workforce in order to make ends meet indicated something was fundamentally broken in our society.

What happened to a peaceful retirement and watching the world go by from your rocking chair? It seemed everyone that breathed was looking for employment. The fact was, there were not enough jobs available for everybody wanting employment.

Recessions are a boom time for companies in areas such as multi-level marketing where a small investment can get someone started. It could take some time to build up a client base and organization substantial enough to support a decent lifestyle through network marketing and some people needed fast money.

Choices were being forced upon individuals they thought they would never have to make. One national news report reported on some highly trained professional women with experience in real estate or finance who had resorted to working as exotic dancers or worse. It seemed applications for those types of jobs had increased nationwide.

Men with advanced degrees were taking any work they could, whether as bartenders or overnight shifts at package shipping companies. Others, in frustration, had turned to desperate acts of crime.

Retailers are enjoying the reliability of older workers who dutifully show up for work and in many cases have elbowed an army of part-time teens to the side. It is not a surprise given the number of baby boomers who have decided to continue working in order to bolster fixed incomes that may not meet their monthly obligations. I noticed senior citizens trying to make ends meet had replaced teenagers behind the counters at fast food restaurants. I saw them and felt their angst. I detected their sense of fatigue from wondering when they could finally sit and rest.

Some of the hardest hit people in this episode are those who were told that their time had passed. Talk of the new economy was code for blue-collar factory workers being obsolete. Where were the displaced automobile workers supposed to go to reclaim their lives? They lived in the midst of some of the most entrenched TARP Towns with massive rates of unemployment, foreclosed homes and shuttered factories. Fear for the future stalked the streets in any city where a heavy manufacture was a major employer.

Finally, there were new faces in line at food banks nationwide. Those new faces were former donors to charities who were forced to ask for help from organizations they once supported. There were bitter pills being swallowed all throughout this land and one of those capsules was pride.

During times such as these it is critical to remember how the individual brings their dignity to the job regardless of title or responsibilities.

There should be a curse on those who pulled us this low while satiating their greed because we were then thrust into the meat grinder of life.

Chapter 15

_____

♦

"Could I get a plain bag, please?"

The prior request became part of the new vocabulary of wealthy individuals trying to enter stealth mode as they exited luxury retail stores. It was no longer fashionable to carry their acquired goods in bags emblazoned with the brand names of the precious cargo they held.

Was this a new age of enlightenment or just another way for the elite to give a wink and nod to each other? Even as they blended in with the masses, they were still above them. There was something unsettling about an almost secret handshake environment of the rich. What would the next step be, private balls sequestered so as to be undiscovered by ordinary peasants. In retrospect, the world of the super rich was already cordoned off from normal society. The only real change was an attempt to shield their visible wealth in order to blend in with society at large.

Some speculated the dressing down and plain shopping bags were signs of sensitivity to the plight of people struggling with the economy. Others felt a sense of self-preservation was the motive lest some frustrated citizens cornered one of the gentry in order to vent their anger.

There was another potential reason for obviously well-heeled people to hide their station in life, guilt. Could it be the exposure of how the accumulation of riches by the few at the top had heaped misery on many others less fortunate than themselves caused them to reflect on their situation?

Why would anyone feel guilty concerning their elevated station in life? The only reason I could envision was if they felt their riches were undeserved. Who would quibble with someone who attained their affluence through providing highly demanded goods or services? I would never begrudge someone who created a company, product or service that filled a void and they profited greatly from it.

Our history is replete with examples of pioneers who changed the nation with their ingenuity. Henry Ford, Bill Gates and Ross Perot all created products that filled a need and made them wealthy individuals. Henry Ford changed the world with the mass produced automobile using the assembly line. Bill Gates changed the world by making the personal computer ubiquitous by creating a de facto standard software platform. Ross Perot pioneered the data processing services industry of selling computing power to industry and government agencies. Those individuals and many others had one thing in common; their affluence came from an exchange of money for something tangible.

Now when we examine the paradox of the wealth generating machine that caused the latest economic crash, there is a void. There were no tangible assets created as a result of billions of dollars flowing into the bank accounts of investment bankers and hedge fund managers. When everything fell apart in October 2008, there was nothing to seize, impound or auction in an attempt to recover any funds. Since all of the actions causing the latest economic problems were legal, there was not even the psychological satisfaction of culprits going to jail. To the contrary we witnessed some of these individuals gain more wealth via multimillion dollar severance packages.

One particularly egregious example of how audacious some of these individuals can be was sale of a $13-million mansion for $100. The eyebrow raising aspect of this sale turned out to be the parties involved in the transaction. It was a deposed investment bank CEO who sold the home to his wife as a preemptive move if legal action ensued against him to recover assets. The execution of such a move seemed to indicate he felt some individual sense of culpability for the nation's financial downfall. Furthermore, if mortgage back security trading was lawful, why take a conspicuous personal action indicating a feeling something took place that might lend itself to some type of recourse through the court system.

Guilt is a strange emotion because individuals cope with it in a wide variety of ways. Some are able to rationalize their actions in a way that mitigates them feeling responsible for the troubles others face. Others deal with guilt effectively by possessing an ability to categorize the affected parties in such a way that makes them seem less than human. The ability to detach is also something many top executives are able to do effectively. It helps to be able to think of others as assets, resources or positions when it was time to displace thousands of them by shutting a plant or consolidating operations to cut costs.

The reality is some of the people have been disconnected from the real world so long that they could be from another planet. I read a lament that was posted online from the wife of an executive whose company received TARP bailout funds from the government. Her great complaint was how she felt constrained by feeling a need to tone down her displays of wealth by being less audacious in her spending. It basically boiled down to splitting hairs between luxurious versus decadent in choices she had to make in clothing and places to throw parties.

Even in the midst of economic chaos, a Wall Street executive managed to scrounge up a $38,000 toilet.

Oh well, so much for cleansing guilt.

Chapter 16

♦

I think it is a worthwhile exercise to examine how certain segments of our economy have changed over the years. When I think back about 40 years ago, we had a retail business landscape driven by largely local, regional and a few national chains. An interesting characteristic of retailers of that era was that they thought of themselves as more specialized ventures. Grocery stores tended to specialize in food and food related items. Department stores like Sears and Montgomery Ward largely handled a variety of dry goods items ranging from clothing to automotive components. In effect, different retail segments generally concentrated on their strengths with a few minor overlaps.

Today's retailers cross many different product categories. The nation's largest seller of groceries and books is the same company, Wal-Mart. Wal-Mart was also ranked as the largest corporation in the world by Fortune Magazine's Global 500 listing for companies whose fiscal year ended on or before March 31, 2008. Of course other companies had to respond to remain competitive. Target Corporation responded with their own version of a superstore called SuperTarget, but they try to sell a slightly higher end product mix than Wal-Mart. Similarly almost every product segment has one or two giant competitors. The warehouse club business is a huge battle between Sam's Club and Costco. Home Improvement center heavyweights Lowes and Home Depot dominate the national scene with a few strong regional chains involved in select geographies. There are similar situations in other retail categories such as home electronics. Chain restaurants have sprawled across the country in fine, casual and fast food. The proliferation of nationwide chains in every category has given the country an anywhere is everywhere feel. Some of the unique character of different regions of the country is gone forever.

How does this situation in retail cause problems during an economic slump? It is the classic multiplier effect of success or failure. Let us examine how some of this has played out during the latest downturn, thus far. Several venerable brands have disappeared from the landscape as operating concerns from a nationwide perspective. The Bombay Company, Linens 'n Things and Circuit City ceased operations as physical store operations in the United States. Other national and regional companies shuttered many locations and are shells of their former selves. Albertsons' grocery stores have closed locations. The company was sold to multiple regional operators and they have since closed many lower performing stores. CompUSA and Bennigan's were vastly different companies, but now they have hundreds of locations closed. Even the juggernaut gourmet-coffee giant Starbucks fell prey to the slowdown as their customers shifted to less expensive options from McDonalds and Dunkin Donuts. Starbucks announced it would close 600 underperforming stores in 2008 and in 2009 the company stated it would shutter an additional 300 locations.

Now let's address the downdraft these companies can create when business conditions get tough. A large chain like Circuit City eliminated 30,000 jobs when it failed. Starbucks announced it would shed 7,000 positions in 2009. Home Depot was shutting down entire divisions that were not part of the core brand such as their high end EXPO Design Centers. When companies with structures like these make adjustments to cut costs, they can terminate thousands of employees with the stroke of a pen. The swift reduction in employment across the country delivered negative shocks to communities. The shocks are often compounded by sometimes large and vacant real estate monuments to the lost positions occupying highly visible locations. Often the derelict stores were the traffic generators other businesses in the same shopping centers depended on for business. It was not unusual for an entire shopping center to end up unoccupied after the anchor tenant locked its doors.

In the old business structure where local and regional stores dominated the landscape, the fallout was limited when the economy went into periods of recession. The closing of 517 stores based upon individual decisions of each store owner across the country versus 517 stores closing at one time as happened with Circuit City illustrate a problem. In the case of the individual owners, some stores might close, others might change strategy and some may be doing fine because their area has a different economic makeup than the nation in general. The logical consensus is the odds of 517 individual businesses ceasing operations at once are not very high. A perfect example is what happened to Bennigan's casual dining restaurants as it went into chapter 7 bankruptcy liquidation and closed approximately 150 company locations. In an odd occurrence, Bennigan's had 150 franchised locations that remained open.

Although the failure of large retailers don't pose the financial danger of a massive bank or AIG going under, it does impose real employment loses and has somewhat of a negative psychological effect on the communities where they operated.

Those large nationwide retail companies came into existence because we, the consumer, made it possible. In a never ending rush to buy products at the lowest possible price, the company that outperformed the others in providing similar products at the lowest cost won. It has been a relentless plunge and at some point there was a wall and it was hit, but not until multiple existing structures and business practices were buried.

Once as many costs were wrung out of the old system as possible the next step was to obtain a lower cost for the product itself. With trade, distance and language barriers irrelevant in the modern context, it was time to go on a world wide sourcing spree for everything from clothing to toys and let the lowest cost provider win. Now you know the reason why many of the products we purchase come from China, Bangladesh and other low-cost-labor centers around the globe. Now when we want to scream at someone for our trade imbalance and questionable product safety, we can do some of our shouting while looking in the mirror every morning. The marathon to be the low-cost provider is almost finished and now we are standing in the valley.

We as consumers could have prevented this but our reasoning that paying the lowest price was always the most logical action led us to this point. We shunned our local merchants who knew us by name and marched into the enclaves owned by those large faceless corporations. Our local wealth which would have all landed in our communities, or at least remained in this country, was siphoned away to distant bank accounts supporting capital creation elsewhere. This has been covered earlier in this book, but our role in bringing about the very thing we abhor cannot be ignored. The cheapest is the best syndrome is something we need a twelve-step program to overcome. How many of us have driven by the skeletons of the past and commented on how things have changed. You know what I am talking about. The used car lot in what was once a hardware store or the unclaimed freight location that formerly housed a family owned furniture store. This is not to cast blame, but to allow us to understand how we are all responsible in some way for what happened to bring us to this point.

I personally don't like wandering around a building large enough to host a football game trying to locate the one thing I came to find. I miss the hardware stores that stocked the 20 percent inventory items the giant superstores don't carry. Admit it, most of us have been in a situation where we needed some out-of-the-ordinary item and went on that joyous search to discover the retailer did not carry it. This is not just something that affects stores like hardware and clothing. There are large specialty retailers in areas like books who are struggling to stay alive. Undoubtedly a large bookstore will carry more selection than a discount store, but the economics break out differently. The pattern of buying 80 percent of your items from a huge discount store usually means a slow death for specialty retailers we run to for the hard to find items. Today the store you know would have that item in stock is either out of business or 10 miles away. Hey, just order it on the internet.

This is not just about the store, but about the origin of the merchandise. I was in a major clothing department store and decided to do an informal survey of where their clothing was manufactured. I think Vietnam took top honors, Costa Rica made a strong showing and of course China was in the mix as well. Some may think I am touting some kind of protectionist policy, but that misses the point. The point is very simple, my late mother once toiled in a sewing factory in my home town of Henderson, Texas. The clothing once created there is probably being manufactured in a low-wage foreign country now. Multiply that situation by the thousands of episodes of shipping those types of jobs to other countries and you have the devastated

United States based clothing and textiles industry. Tens of thousands of Americans lost their employment when production for clothing   moved   offshore.

Chapter 17

♦

Our self-image is quite different from current reality. I think we live in a mental time warp of who we were as a country many years ago. Our manufacturing base was strong and the world clamored for American made products. When we traveled abroad, foreigners were eager to please the visitors from the United States. Let us strip away the illusion we have lived in for at least the last twenty years. Our manufacturing base has been largely destroyed by foreign outsourcing. We now ship out raw materials that come back into this country as finished goods. We import food, clothing and many advanced-technology products.

Our economy has become one largely based upon retail and service industries. In other words we have moved from being the great producers to the mass consumers. How many restaurants, movie theatres and department stores does one country need?

American based companies steeped in history such as Macy's, J.C. Penny and Wal-Mart may own those outlets, but they are a collective foreign bazaar funneling billions of dollars to locales around the globe.

Americans have become concentrated in what I call zones of dependence. People packed into cities and suburbs depend on the local supermarket, water department and electric utility company for everything they need to survive. The lure of the industrial economy changed the way people in America approached life. The exodus of young people from small towns became a right of passage as they felt that was where their career opportunities resided. In the process millions of people became concentrated within concrete deserts that yielded very little that was not brought in to sustain the masses. The weakness of these cities is often exposed when severe economic downturns come along. Job losses are often much higher in urban areas when large plants shut down and leave former employees stranded inside paved wastelands. That is why comparisons of this downturn to the Great Depression miss the mark. That was a different nation with heartier individuals who possessed what I believe were better survival skills. A family could till the soil and grow food to sustain them in hard times. We are not an agricultural economy anymore. Today we are urban and suburban creatures who are much more fragile. We don't know the corner grocer who might start an account because he knew your family or barter meat for vegetables grown in your garden. A nationwide chain store could not care less about how much you have spent with them in the past if you are down on you luck. "Get out or get arrested", would be their reply.

We have to redouble our efforts and support those taking a chance by starting a small business. You already know their goods will cost more than at the 200,000 square foot superstore, but that is how we got into the situation we are in now. There was a television commercial illustrating the problem; a not so loyal customer told a banker who had transacted business with the guy for years that the bank could bid to do his new home loan. It seemed clever at the time, but going with the lowest bidder is the attitude that got into this situation to begin with. The guy with the lowest starter interest rate got the home loan or the builder who threw in the most upgrades earned the house sale. One thing we now understand clearly is there is no such thing as something for nothing.

We talk a lot about how small businesses are the engine driving the economy, but do we put our money where our mouths are. Why don't you write down the local companies in your memory that you once patronized that are no longer around. If you are under twenty years old, your idea of local retailers is probably the mega-stores you grew up with. Now think about reality and imagine swimming upstream trying to start a new venture when the trusted names belong to industry giants. We have to reevaluate the effect our dollars have when we spend them and who we spend them with.

Chapter 18

♦

We no longer lived in isolation and what happens to our economy has ramifications worldwide. Many nations had direct damage to their financial systems because their banks and investment banks invested in mortgage-backed collateralized debt obligations. Those nations have had economic issues similar to the United States although to varying degrees of severity.

Banking is a worldwide marketplace. Companies do not care what country a bank is based in when they are seeking investment capital. The same can be said for the banks themselves when it comes to seeking out worthwhile projects to invest in. All that really matters is getting the required financial returns and that knows no boundaries. It is that borderless business boundary that allowed the worldwide enmeshments of the mortgage backed security trading business. Once the international investments were made it was a commitment for both the upside and downside of the performance of the MBS vehicles. Only now are some of the foreign institutions left wondering if what they bought was of the quality represented by Wall Street. Now we can see why accusatory fingers were pointed in our direction from across vast oceans. Many of the problems other countries experienced due to our recession were due to the collapse of consumer demand for their exported products. As an example Toyota experienced sales drops up to 40 percent monthly over prior year similar periods.

There is one foreign occurrence I feel is directly related to our economic downturn, but I have yet to hear anyone else make a connection. There has been a dramatic surge in drug violence in Mexico near the United States border.

My case is that one of the first industries to fall was construction when the mortgage crisis hit full force. Many of Mexican descent were employed in the building trade and when that collapsed, a great source of income dried up almost overnight. It has been repeatedly reported that one of the largest revenue sources going into Mexico were dollars from people in the United States sending money back to relatives. Incomes that took a hit from construction and other industries going down may have caused a drop in money flowing into Mexico. There was violence in the drug trade there before, but I feel those cartels are chasing fewer dollars for their products and are fighting to eliminate competition. I could be completely off base, but it is not an unfamiliar pattern for slimmer times to cause greater competition for fewer resources.

Chapter 19

♦

We were all getting dizzy from hearing about what has happened and I don't think anyone really wanted to tell us what really transpired. The stock market went down to levels hard to imagine a few years ago when it seemed the only direction was up.

The issue of the stock market points out how this crisis is viewed by different factions in our country. By listening to the broadcast media in this nation, one would think this is a problem that will be cured if the stock market simply goes back up. The stock market going up will help the value of investments in the stock market which would include many 401k and other retirement accounts.

The following is a quick demystification of the stock market. The stock market is where shares are bought and sold representing the value of various publicly traded companies. When a corporation issues new stock, the stock market is the marketplace used to present that security to potential investors for purchase in order to raise money for the company to operate. All other monetary transactions in the stock of a company already trading on a stock exchange does not go to the company, but to the owner of the stock who sold it. That means nearly all of the shares of stock bought and sold every day, is trading between one party selling to another with the company the security represents having no part in the exchange. The instances when a company participates in the trading of it own stock is if it decides to repurchase its own shares, issue more shares or has an initial public offering.

When you look at the stock market in that light, it seems to decline in significance unless it has a direct impact on you. Now when the markets decline as much as they have recently, there is a large decrease in the net worth of individuals, investments and companies. You have to understand the decline in net worth only becomes concrete if the stock is sold at the lower value. If the stock is held and the stock prices recover then there was a temporary on paper. The one caveat is if a company goes through a bankruptcy which often cancels the common stock of investors.

There are times when the decrease in stock prices could pose a problem even when they are not sold and that is if it is pledged as collateral to secure debt. For many people a stock market crash is a very emotional event, but in some cases it may be completely irrelevant to their day-to-day lives.

So why are stock traders so up in arms? Traders make money by executing transactions that generate fees. When stocks decline in value, investors often flee to other forms of investments such as commodities or bonds. The stock market is often viewed as a financial barometer and the shrill shouts from financial reporters and shouting headlines tend to generate a sense of panic in the general public. If a company is solid, has tangible assets and a secure place in its industry, the stock price will be less of a reflection of the health of the firm during a recession.

One thing to remember about the stock market is that it can be a contrary indicator as it relates to how good news is for workers. As an example a stock may go up because a company announces that it is laying off thousands of employees. The reason the stock goes up is because a workforce reductions could mean lower costs and increased profits to the bottom line. That is why institutional investors may watch the stock market with one set of eyes while those not involved look at the ups and downs in a totally different light.

Unless you are invested in the stock market and plan to sell your stock in the short term, it is probably a good idea to refrain from watching every up and down movement. You will sleep much better and by all means, turn those screaming television heads off, because they did not see this coming either.

Chapter 20

♦

Just how serious is this crisis and how do we pull out of it?

I can only tell you about what I see, feel and hear. At the age of 50 I have been through several downturns. The oil embargo and a downturn in the early eighties that chased me from Tyler, Texas to Dallas when the oil economy died, were serious economic upheavals, but they paled when compared to this recession.

This situation was an almost perfect alignment of negative factors with industries affected across the board and it was hard to escape the path of destruction. Let's walk through some of the problem areas.

Construction was an immediate victim because new home construction took a nosedive as the mortgage business collapsed and home foreclosures rose. Homebuilders have failed across the country.

The mortgage industry took a huge hit in new home loan financing. Subprime lending companies went out of business when that segment of mortgage lending disappeared. IndyMac bank, one of the nation's largest mortgage lenders failed. Bank of America acquired Countywide Financial Corporation which was the nation's largest morgtgage company. Refinancing of current home loans is still an active niche and some provisions of the economic stimulus package should boost it even more.

Investment banking was crippled with the major players emerging as divisions of other companies, instead of remaining independent entities as they were before, or became bank holding companies. Those companies were at the tip of the spear in trading mortgage-backed securities. When the market collapsed, the investment banks fell with them. The only investment bank to be completely liquidated was Lehman-Brothers. The surreal scene of Lehman-Brothers employees lined up on the sidewalk outside of the corporate headquarters on a weekend night with boxes to collect their personal effects sent a chill down my spine. It looked like an updated scene from the Great Depression except it was the year 2008. Merrill Lynch was merged with Bank of America. The last two major investment banks in the United States, Goldman-Sachs and Morgan-Stanley will become bank holding companies. These companies had been in existence for more than 150, 100, 90 and 70 years. Each in their own way ceased to exist in their prior forms due to the recession that began in 2007.

State and local governments have been reeling under the weight of this downturn. Shrinking property tax revenues due to declining home values, lower sales tax revenue due to decreased buying and dwindling unemployment compensation funds because of job losses are causing hard decisions on service cutbacks. Most state governments have balanced budget requirements in their state constitutions and the only way to achieve their goals were employment and service reductions. Some states are running deficits into the tens of billions of dollars. California went on a program of mandatory unpaid days off for state employees to save on payroll. Some cities are closing library branches, reducing trash pick up days and laying off teachers. Some police forces were having issues bringing officers onto the payroll who had completed their training academies.

The problem with retailers was one of decreased spending and a shift in spending to basics such as food. There has also been a shift downward to lower price retailers. Some of the winners here are Wal-Mart and other discount stores. Big ticket products such as higher end electronics and furniture have been hit hard. The simple fact is replacing items such as furniture and appliances are often choices instead of necessities. Automobile dealers who sell the second most expensive item most people will buy are experiencing an especially difficult time. Tight credit and weak demand have combined to cause several large dealerships to close their doors, often leaving customer in the lurch. Many more small dealers have shut down their operation in virtual silence. In May of 2009, GM announced that it would close 1,100 dealers while Chrysler said it would shed 789 dealers. That is a blow to the business owners, communities and poses a service headache for many owners of those cars who will have to travel longer distances to reach service departments.

The restaurant sector is experiencing softness as customers cut back on how often they go out. When people do eat out during tough times they may trade down to less expensive options. Many casual dining chains have introduced lower cost items, two-for-one meals and other enticements to attract diners who are watching their spending.

Service companies providing everything from printing, home services and hair care experienced a reduction in demand for their work. Whether it was delaying a large direct mail campaign or women stretching out the time between hair salon visits, it all had a cumulative negative revenue effect. Instead of a sharp decline, stretching out intervals of spending had a slow erosive effect on the ability of companies to remain viable. One of my barometers was my daily mail delivery. There were days when I had no sales flyers, post card offers or printed personalized promotional offers delivered by my postman. Those printed pieces were the lifeblood of some printing company that was experiencing a decline in their business.

Banking was an uneven story depending on how much exposure an individual institution had in the subprime mortgage and mortgage backed security collapse. The real problems are coming due to the credit lockup that was making it difficult for banks to even lend to each other. Credit card default risks are a looming problem as more people lose their jobs. Wells Fargo now owns Wachovia. The government owns 40 percent of Citigroup after it lost out in a tug of war with J P Morgan to acquire Washington Mutual. Various banks have received billions in federal bailout funds to shore up their balance sheets in an attempt to restart business and consumer lending.

Heavy manufacturing of passenger vehicles and construction equipment are both in a slowdown. With demand down for new car purchases, the automobile companies both foreign and domestic have had to take drastic actions to adjust production to meet lower unit sales. General Motors and Chrysler have both accepted billions in government loans. Both automobile companies are reducing shifts, closing plants and eliminating brands to cut cost and increase efficiency. Construction equipment manufacturers have a similar problem because a slowdown in all forms of construction reduces the need for their products. Caterpillar, the world's largest construction equipment company has laid off thousands of employees.

Even the recyclable material market has been affected. An oversupply of recyclable materials due to people redeeming paper, cardboard and metals for cash have swamped recycling centers. A drop in demand because of the slowdown in manufacturing has caused some to stop turning in items because they feel the price they bring is not worth departing with the material. Some have decided to wait until prices recover before turning in their collection of goods to a recycling center.

Some businesses will prosper even during an economic downturn. Pawnshop operators were doing well as people turned in various items for pawn loans. Companies in the automobile repossession business had a booming trade. Healthcare was also holding its own as sickness transcends the economy, however more of the care given was for uninsured patients due to unemployment. Unfortunately companies providing services to clear foreclosed homes of their former occupants abandoned possessions were so busy they could barely keep up.

With a few exceptions, you could almost play name that industry and figure out how the recession had affected their business prospects. There is a strange deceptiveness about this recession an it is difficult to determine reality from illusions. Suddenly it seemed that banks transferred from near death to suddenly earning billions of dollars in profit in one quarter, but was it real. There was a change in an accounting rule that most in the general public didn't notice. Something called mark-to-market accounting required banks to value assets such as bad loans at the rate they could be sold to buyers in real time. With so many bad assets with little to no set value, banks were in a loss position. After intense lobbying the mark-to-market rule was changed and banks could then revalue nonperforming assets based upon more favorable probable circumstances. After the accounting rule change, suddenly multiple banks reported surprising profits. Were the instant profits real or another smoke and mirrors routine?

Chapter 21

———————————————————————

♦

Who was running the show? There was a real question of who was more powerful, the sovereign government of the United States of American or a group of massive financial corporations who were able to take the world economy hostage and demand unheard of ransom payments.

This was the dilemma the country found itself in when cries that the financial sky was falling started to sound from the hallowed halls of Wall Street firms. The call was if the taxpayers did not save them, their demise would bring everyone else down with them.

I want to paint a picture of what has happened to the taxpayers of this country as clearly as I can.

Imagine you walked outside of your home to go to work in the morning. You heard a noise behind you and before you could react, someone placed a cloth over your nose and you passed out. When you woke up, you realized you were outside, naked and your money was gone. You looked up and the person who robbed you was standing there with all of your possessions. You were stunned because there was no attempt to escape or even hide his face.

"Who are you?"

"I am a Wall Street investment banker?" he replied.

"Why did you take all of my stuff?"

"I didn't mean for you to find out about this? I was using your mortgage to make money by selling it to other people, but when you couldn't keep up with the payments after it adjusted upward, I had no choice but to come to you directly," the banker replied.

"I don't know you. I never gave you permission to sell my mortgage."

"Look, I've got other stops to make. I'll see you later," the banker says as he got into a car worth more than your house.

You suddenly realized you were standing outside naked and ran to your front door. Your key would not open the door as the locks had been changed. An eviction notice was taped to your window and a sense of panic washed over you

After scraping together enough money to get a hotel room and new clothes, you finally managed to get an apartment one fifth the size of your former home. After two weeks of living in your new location, you

147

heard a noise behind you and before you can react, someone placed a cloth over your nose and you passed out. When you woke up, you realized you were outside, naked and your money was gone. You looked up and the same person that robbed you before was standing there again with all of your possessions. This time you were outraged and called the authorities.

Before you could fully describe the situation the person on the other end of the line told you this was happening to everyone and you should not be alarmed. You were told the next time you saw this person, just hand over your money and everything would be fine. You replied that all of your money was gone. It turned out not to be a problem because the government had agreed on a plan with the bankers to pay all of them from loans taken out in everybody's name because it was more efficient.

You are stunned and asked why you needed to pay money to strangers. The answer explained how investment banks got into trouble trading mortgage backed securities and needed a bailout because if they failed, the economy could go down with them. You were also informed about a giant insurance company, AIG, that needed a bailout also because they insured the mortgage backed securities the bankers sold. The explanation was when people like you couldn't make their subprime mortgage payments the whole thing collapsed and AIG did not have adequate reserves to pay those quasi-insurance policies called credit default swaps.

You are livid. How dare they blame all of this chaos on you? Even if you made a mistake and bought a house you couldn't afford, it was a personal mistake. You did not tell these investment bankers and insurance companies to build a huge financial monster on top of your home loan. If your home went into foreclosure, it should have been between you and your original mortgage company. These banks, insurance companies and investment banks were no more than financial squatters who used rules originally constructed to dispose of toxic assets from a prior savings & loan failure to enrich themselves. This time those rules were used recklessly and create a far larger collapse.

Chapter 22

♦

The outrages will continue. Hundreds of millions of dollars in bonuses for AIG executives for selling financial products the company could not back up seemed outrageous. An insolvent Citigroup, that was existing on billions in taxpayer funds, spent millions to place their name on a baseball stadium and millions more to remodel executives' offices. The litany of excesses could go on forever. The problem was an ingrained sense of entitlement.

Worlds collided in the most unusual of circumstances. The financially elite have to come to grips with a new reality. The reality was the sheltered world they lived in was revealed for all to see. The money, luxuries and self-indulgence had been laid bare and the reaction was revulsion instead of reverence. As people found themselves out of their homes, jobs and lifestyles, they saw the result of unchecked upward wealth redistribution.

Regular citizens found wealth that went up, never trickled back down.

There is a tendency for a few with huge excesses of wealth to be far less beneficial to the economy than many with an equitable amount to live on. The many I speak of was the vibrant middle class that for decades comprised the heart of this nations economy. A country with a strong and vast middle class will produce more, consume more and have an economy less prone to drastic swings upward or downward.

The middle class in this country has been under assault for years. One of the bedrocks ensuring a strong foundation for the country was manufacturing which has been severely downgraded in the United States. There is an extreme amount of wealth concentrated with people who have created nothing tangible other than the organizations sustaining their businesses of trading various financial instruments.

Think about what is really going on in a securities market. Follow the path of a stock trading on the market. A share of XYZ starts the day at $10 per share, it goes up to $11 and owner #1 sells and makes $1 per share. Owner #2 shorts the stock betting it will go down and it sells it at $10 and he makes $1 per share. Owner #3 sells the stock at $11 and makes $1 per share. Three people have made $1 off the same share of stock. Multiply that $1 by 10,000 shares and each person made

$10,000 off the same stock. Was anything tangible created by trading in that stock, no? Did the company represented by the stock receive any of the funds generated by the trading, no? What really happened here was a series of electronic transactions occurred where the difference in the buy and sale price generated money with no actual real wealth creation. That is the story of stock market trading. Fortunes are made and lost daily based upon many factors including luck. If this sounds suspiciously like gambling then you are not far off the mark.

When you really think about it, the best parallel is horse racing. You find out as much as you can about the horse/company. You hope there is not anything going on with the horse/company you don't know about. Surprises for a racehorse may be a injured leg occurring during warm-up. A company may have a pending product recall that will send the stock price down when it is announced. So you thought the stock market was more complex than that, well it is. There are licenses, certifications and other requirements if you want to be on-site at the market executing trades from the floor. Some investors use technical analysis and ratios to guide their trading activity. However you can execute stock transactions from the comfort of your home from a computer by simply opening up an account with an online brokerage company, funding your account and selecting the companies you want to place your bet on. The difference between you being in the market and the Wall Street guys, is they play with millions of dollars.

Living in an economic world foreign to the average American creates a huge disconnect between citizens. One group's normal is another's idea of wretched excess. Now is the time to end the fairy tale and bring everything back into balance.

Chapter 23

♦

We were pumping taxpayer funds into banks and AIG on such a massive scale that many individuals and politicians were reaching high levels of anxiety. Why was it so critical for these institutions to survive that the nation seemed willing to mortgage its future to insure those firms continued to function.

What most people in the general public does not know would probably give them more sleepless nights than what we do know. The future behind the scenes issues inside the banks are comprised of some of the same problems that brought the economy down to begin with, but in the form of commercial real estate securitized investment vehicles. That is a secondary item that could emerge if the economy sunk the commercial real estate market and loans financing the purchase of office buildings, plants and shopping centers started to go into default.

154

We could have a second round of credit default swap calls that would pile on top of the residential loan default problem. Guess what, those commercial real estate loan bonds were used just like residential to create CDO instruments.

I believe an effort to prevent round two of the first collapse is a motivating factor in keeping these financial institutions afloat.

How many more shoes are out there waiting to drop? How about credit card loan defaults? Prolonged unemployment will bring that issue to the forefront. As you can see, there are a collection of problems that could still spring out from under the cover of the banking debacle.

AIG is not a bank but it seems to be the face of the downturn of 2008. The reason AIG is in the center of this meltdown is because it is almost acting as a clearing house with links to most of the institutions out there that were deep into trading of those mortgage backed securities.

Due to the amount of CDS acquired by investors to hedge against default of mortgage backed securities, AIG is almost a distribution point for bailout funds. When billions in taxpayer funds flowed into AIG, billions flowed out to companies like Citigroup and Goldman Sachs to pay claims due to MBS defaults.

Unfortunately we seem to be locked into a game of endurance to see what exhausts itself first, our patience or our credit line with China. Of course the government has the authority to created money by increasing the money supply. We will pay for that later with higher inflation.

Another point of contention is why the banks and AIG seem to be getting better treatment than the automakers. Is it really class related or is it something deeper?

There are some parallels we could draw. One is like losing an arm and the other is losing your heart.

The automakers are vital to the functioning of the country from a manufacturing capability standpoint. Millions of jobs are tied to the building of vehicles in this country. The car manufacturers in many ways are victims of the recession, but losing GM or Chrysler would be a tragedy. Losing our banking system would be a catastrophe.

The banking system is the oil, gas and battery our country runs on. Without a functioning banking system in place many business functions in this country would seize up and simply stop. Without financing for inventory, payroll and many other activities many companies would have to cease operations. Even if a company is operating on a break even basis, it is still supporting jobs and paying employees. Many in that category would be the first to go down if the banking system shut down.

Now to AIG, aside from the financial products division, it is a massive insurance company. If AIG failed what would happen to businesses using them for coverage. Would business locations be able to open and allow employees and customers onto their sites without insurance coverage?

So just get a policy from another carrier, right. Remember earlier when I described credit default swaps as quasi-insurance policies without sufficient assets backing them to pay in full. Insurance companies are required to maintain a certain asset to risk ratio on actual insurance coverage it issues. One problem the market could face might be an asset issue for other insurance companies' ability to absorb the customers from a company as large as AIG.

Another problem would be the disruption that could occur as customers scrambled to replace their coverage. There is another big issue sitting out there and it is huge numbers of people have AIG policies covering their life, cars and homes. If AIG is gone, who pays the claims?

AIG was a study in how a company could become so entangled in multiple aspects of the global financial system that simply figuring out what impact its failure would have was difficult to determine. When investment banks failed at an alarming rate, I don't really know if anyone anticipated how pivotal a role an insurance company played in the debacle.

Chapter 24

♦

It is time to do what many would have thought unimaginable a few years ago, break those massive institutions down into smaller component parts. Some will scream, "Let the free enterprise system function". We have tried that and in the modern context it does not work very well and I will go through a few reasons why.

Hired managers with no creation capital invested in the organization run most of the large companies today. What I mean by creation capital is someone that started the business or is a descendant of the founders. A sense of personal responsibility for a company and its effect on society was something most founders felt for their creation. Henry Ford thought Ford Motor Company was an extension of what he stood for. After a company has been in business for generations and outside CEOs are brought in with bonus structures based upon increasing short-term gross profits and earnings per share, then that becomes the goal. The long term viability of the business takes a secondary role to the current quarter's profit. If shutting a plant down in the United States and moving production to Vietnam increases quarterly profits, the move is likely to occur. The fact that long tenured company employees would lose their jobs became a necessary evil less important than reaching the quarterly profit target.

Corporate officers with their compensation tied to stock options created a hot house environment designed to pump up share prices. Golden parachutes guaranteeing top executive massive payouts if they were dismissed from their posts, did little to instill motivation to think long term.

AIG, Countrywide Financial, Washington Mutual, Fannie Mae, Freddie Mac, Wachovia, Bear Stearns, Citigroup and Merrill Lynch are companies that in one way or another failed during the latest financial crisis. The Chief Executive Officers of the firms listed before, exited their organizations as they were crashing with an estimated combined $583 million in golden parachute and stock payouts. The CEO of one other firm Lehman Brothers which failed completely, reportedly received nearly one half billion dollars in pay between 1993 and 2007

What is abundantly clear is how these corporate titans live in a different world than the rest of us. They operate on a different plane than those who are merely wealthy. These executives live in the rarified air of a group of people who can do practically anything they want, whenever they choose because cost is not an obstacle. What is so curious about most of these people is their activity of choice is to add to their incredible mounds of money and what they can acquire with their wealth.

There is a huge gulf starting to be bridged between the corporate aristocracy and the average person. As more of the naked avarice and excess became exposed, the lower in public esteem these villains fell. Those once regarded as geniuses were viewed in a new light. How fast the mighty have fallen. We can't ever allow them to again reach those lofty heights they once inhabited. By perpetrating schemes that showed disregard for their fellow man all in the pursuit of riches beyond reason, the glow of the end justifying the means has severely dimmed.

This crisis was the greatest teaching tool this country had to discredit the philosophy of "get it while you can" as a way to live your life. What we all thought was a near nirvana of economic growth really turned out to be a parasitic system feeding upon itself. Once the host that kept this mass freeloading pyramid intact began to falter, there was not enough economic lifeblood to sustain the parasite and it collapsed. Because the immense wealth amassed by trading these mortgage derivatives was not based upon creating actual tangible assets, it simply vanished into thin air and into the bank accounts of Wall Street executives. The problem was while these parasitic entities, like common ticks, would detach after they were engorged, the unsuspecting host may have been crippled depending on how much blood it had lost. While the host was struggling to survive, the parasite was lying in wait for another unfortunate, innocent victim to come along. As it turned out in this case the bloodsuckers were feeding upon several hosts at once including mortgage holders, investors in their companies and their employers. That was the ultimate irony; this frenzy was the equivalent of burning down your own house to stay warm in the winter. Sadly, a new host was found and it was the American taxpayers.

Amazingly, science fiction became reality. Many of the investment firms, banks and insurance companies died from injuries due to the economic crash and have become the living dead. Citigroup, AIG, Fannie Mae and Freddie Mac had been reanimated and were sustained by umbilical cords attached to the federal government that kept their vital signs stable. Even though the very survival of these companies was dependant upon life giving infusions of funds from the taxpayers' coffers, some of the executives still behaved the same as when their companies operated under their own steam. Just like Frankenstein's monster, they had to be retrained before angry mobs descended upon them with torches and pitchforks. Several got the message after being stung by bitter comments coming from those long thought to be beneath their station in life. Others feared becoming pariahs who would become outcasts confined to their gilded castles. A select few simply feared the worst. Some employed security services to guard their property and person. AIG was in the center of a populist backlash so severe that the company's CEO said the company's name would probably be changed. Most of the anger focused against AIG revolved around $165 million dollars of retention bonus payments to executives in the companies Financial Products Division.

In addition to breaking some of these companies up into smaller units, safeguards must be enacted to make it difficult for any single firm to become large enough to be in a position to destroy the nation's and possibly the world's economy.

Regulators must inspect what they expect from companies doing business in financial markets. Just printing rules and regulations that are not enforced, simply encourages widespread abuse. If more enforcement manpower is needed, then fund it with additional fees from the trading activity on Wall Street.

The musical chairs game of investment banking executives moving into the United States Treasury Department must end. There has been too much familiarity between the heads of large investment banks and government officials whose task it was to regulate an industry run by former colleagues. We end up with strange situations of government officials in charge of untangling financial disasters that may have began when they were running the very companies creating the problem. How can the public trust someone to admit being part of the problem they are trying to rectify?

As with any cycle involving predator and prey in nature there is a need for scavengers to dispose of the remains. Nature has many efficient examples patrolling the land, sky and seas. We also have financial scavengers that will scoop up the residue of these failed financial products and sort through them. Over time, the waste from of this debacle will disappear from the economic landscape just as the Great Depression did, but never from our memory.

Why do we keep making the same mistakes?

One line of thought is the serial economic calamities that keep befalling us may not be unintentional. The last few years the American public was in a state of continual distraction. Crafty politicians and special interest groups have kept the population screaming at each over cultural, religious and other hot button issues while very well dressed scam artists have looted our coffers. As we argued about same-sex marriage, abstinence and any other third rail topic that changed the subject, our future was being stolen. Thieves have long known that mayhem brings opportunity. A riot or blackout invites looting that makes for compelling video scenes of people running with televisions hoisted on their shoulders. The chaos of war is ripe for profiteering by those trading in the tools of war and we know it first hand from the examples of Halliburton, Blackwater and KBR Brown and Root in Iraq. Economic turmoil creates a similar chaotic environment where money and financial transactions are difficult to track and understand. It is in these environments where fortunes are made and lost in the blink of an eye. In the midst of the financial confusion, some families found themselves crammed in with other relatives after they had lost their homes. Some are now living in shelters, on the streets and even in 21st century tent cities that I called TARP Towns earlier in this book. It has come to this. I urge all individuals to beware when some issue forces its way to the forefront in order to divert our collective attention because there is a much larger transgression taking place behind the scenes.

We need to apply the lessons learned from our repeated downfalls and focus on what really matters. When you are out of work, homeless or your retirement fund is empty, what other people do in their personal lives does not seem to matter as much, does it?

Chapter 25

♦

The United States will emerge from this downfall as a country that will once again lead the world instead of being in a totally dependent posture. We will transform ourselves into a haven of innovation and production instead of being known for mass consumerism. This will only happen after going through a period of detoxification and painful withdrawals just like anyone coming off of a chronic drug addiction. Our drugs of choice were greed, arrogance and excess. Our culture was saturated with a doctrine that the over class deserved every material indulgence they could get their hands on. In fact a brand of religion sprung up to reinforce the point even when they went to church, prosperity gospel. If many were armed with a belief they had a divine right to material wealth, how was logic going to creep in and prevent them from getting in over their heads financially. Others were swept up in a frenzy of expectations causing them to be open to overreaching and became overextended in the matters of finance. There was a delusional state existing on streets and drives across the country of being among the big fish in the pond. Suddenly those so called big fish noticed a large shadow coming up from below. All too late, a realization set in that they had drifted from their quaint ponds and found themselves in the midst of a deep ocean. After being rounded up, into what is called a bait ball in nature, the huge shape from the depths opened its enormous mouth and swallowed the small fish whole. The monster was one of the true financial whales who devoured all in their path and such was the fate of many who thought they had reached the summit of the American dream. It was all a grand delusion.

The overarching issue that must be addressed is the loss of empathy for others in our country and in the world. Did any of these security traders consider what could happen to the dreams of millions of their fellow Americans if their complex investment vehicles failed and crippled the financial system? The shrapnel flew off in all directions and sent multiple sectors of the economy crashing and caused numerous casualties far removed from the Wall Street disaster. Almost every segment of the economy was suffering due to weakened demand, real job losses, tepid consumer confidence and fear of what may come. As the government dealt with the nation in crisis, it was akin to a doctor trying to save a patient with multiple organs failing at the same time.

I will end this chapter with advice that, if followed, may prevent this national festival of national pain from repeating itself.

Before you undertake any action in the future, answer the following questions.

Will the best possible outcome only benefit you? Will the worst possible outcome hurt others?

If the answer to the prior questions is yes, don't do it.

Chapter 26

♦

Americans will have to become a more curious group of people. We are set to enter a new age of darkness as it relates to knowing about critical news development that affects our daily lives. With several major city newspapers either bankrupt or teetering on the edge of insolvency, we may be forced to rely on television or internet driven news sources. While some may think the 24-hour access and instant update nature of those electronic mediums are far more current than constantly outdated newspaper print formats, but there is a huge deficiency missed by most people.

Local television driven news programming is time constrained and only presents a few top stories at its best. Once commercial breaks are added into the equation a local 30-minute newscast is probably only 15 to 20 minutes of actual news programming. Once time is subtracted for the sports and weather segment, how much actual news content is left. Cable news is a highly scripted and almost an infotainment format. Some cable news channels repeat the same show format hour after hour with only a few new breaking stories per day. If a viewer switches between cable networks, they will often find the same stories being covered with identical video feeds on the screen.

Seattle Washington could become the first large American city without a major print newspaper as the Seattle Post-Intelligencer ceased its print publication and became an exclusively online entity. The remaining print newspaper, the Seattle Times, was in a struggle for survival. If a large city did not have a major newspaper, a section of the population that was not online or computer savvy could go into a relative blackout when it came to in-depth news coverage. As is often the case, older, less educated and lower-income sectors of the population are more likely to be in the dark.

The 137-year old Boston Globe was in a fight for its life as its owner the New York Times Company threatened to close the daily newspaper down. The entire future of the newspaper business is in question due to several dynamics including lower advertising revenue, declining circulation and competition from free information sources on the internet. Newspapers are a labor and capital intensive business. Newspapers have huge expenses involved in physical plant, press equipment and distribution. Given the different economies of scale between a daily print publication compared to a successful online blog and there is no comparison.

Why don't television and the internet fill the void? Much of what is on cable is affected by point-of-view programming dictated by the network ownership. Fox News, CNN and MSNBC by most accounts would all be categorized as having an ideological stance affecting their news coverage. The second issue is depth. Newspapers are known for having reporters and bureaus covering wide areas of interest. Most large metropolitan newspapers have reporters assigned to cover city government, crime, business, local happenings and much more. Knowing what is going on at the city council meeting may be much more important than tracking a celebrity divorce scandal. Newspapers could delve deeply into issues and were limited by the access to information and not by time. If a story was not completed in one day's edition it could be continued in the next daily publication.

The internet has content with seemingly no end, but who is able to verify the veracity of the sources. Anyone can blog, post and distribute anything online and there is no way to authenticate the accuracy of the information.

The bottom line is in the post-crash era, everyone will need to ask second and third level questions about information presented to them. Although it appears we are in the midst of an information explosion, much of it is pure quantity and not much quality.

Chapter 27

♦

I am of the opinion that upheavals whether social or economic have a corresponding cost expressed on the other side. The economic collapse that emerged in 2008 certainly had a social counterpart that built up over the same period of time.

The relentless pursuit of material wealth that led to the latest recession had to express itself with a negative societal cost. Now it is time to briefly visit the social recession resulting from the actions that created the economic downturn. Some may say this is just the ramblings of a layman, but I'll quote a law of nature that seems to be constant in almost every aspect of life and that law is every action has an equal and opposite reaction.. Aristotle's idiom stating how nature abhors a vacuum also has some application. I am of the opinion that the world is comprised of two types of economic wealth, active and latent. Active wealth is what man has the means to transform into what he views as useful and latent wealth is beyond mans ability to convert into something useful. An example is nuclear power which is now useful after man discovered how to harness the power of the atom. Conversely a new exploitation of wealth may obsolete a previously valuable stalwart as the automobile did with the horse and buggy. On a larger scale there is economic wealth and social wealth.

With so many involved in the pursuit of financial success there was almost no way to escape a downturn in our social fortunes. Much of the cultural downturn manifested itself within our younger citizens. Values were driven in many cases by popular culture figures, who in many cases, had little to validate their fame. An oddity is modern notoriety driven fame that would have faded quickly in prior years was now sustained by relentless tabloid and mainstream media coverage. The era of constant news feeding the celebrity machine had arrived. The old notions of infamy had been cast aside and it seemed no wrongs could tarnish the celebrity adoration felt by fans.

Scandals created some of the era's brightest stars. Celebrity sex-video scandals became one of the sure ways to cement lasting fame short of an actual marketable talent. The formula seemed to include a semi-famous name or noteworthy acquaintances, video recorded sexual tryst and celebrity coverage about a leak of a sex tape. Usually this rumored tape never surfaced until an appropriately lucrative contract was struck with a distributor. Once the tape was in the public domain, the stars would do a few contrite interviews and move on to do reality television shows. The public's near insatiable appetite for sideshows have rewarded some of the worst behavior with handsome financial payoffs. Somehow a career path of being the-life-of-the-party was created and the ability to draw crowds of curious onlookers apparently paid well.

Even serious charges against our antisocial heroes failed to dim their popularity. Various luminaries have faced serious accusations such driving under the influence, child molestation and assault. Despite the aforementioned troubles the adoring public seemed to have a deep well of forgiveness and continued to elevate their heroes and rewarded them with even greater fame and fortune.

Given those prior examples it was little wonder that fans of that generation would try to emulate the activities of their role models. Troubling behaviors such as teens sending text messages from their cellular phones containing nude images of themselves to their friends were becoming commonplace. Drinking alcohol, drug use and engaging in sexual activity at younger ages than ever, were some of the symptoms of our social bankruptcy that mirrored our economic insolvency.

New scourges appeared on the scene like methamphetamines to go along with old standbys like crack and power cocaine. Life was a minefield for parents attempting to steer their children in a more traditional direction from a social and career standpoint. Among the older-hero set the infraction of late seemed to be tax evasion, insider trading and lying to federal investigators. Those earning millions of dollars appeared to find it necessary to retain even more by skipping out on their federal tax obligations. Lest we forget the parade of marital affairs, dalliances with prostitutes and steroid laced supermen of the mature set.

Those of us who are more mature did not escape our part in the social downfall. Remember the 10-year age slip campaign, 50 is the new 40, etc. The prior years had been the age of vanity. Artificially enhanced lips, hips and pectoral muscles were all symptoms of a refusal to grow old gracefully. That desire to hang on to youth also permeated into the thinking of those individuals to act 10 years younger than their chronological age. Mothers and fathers acting more like their children's friends than parents caused a breakdown of normal role model behavior. If mom and dad were always out on the town then how could they tell their children to act more responsibly?

It remains to be seen, but the country's economic problems could serve to focus the attention of the nation on the need to pull back to a saner social harbor. Adults have to take their place as the true role models for those that are younger. Frustration could set in as luxuries that young people became accustomed to move out of reach. Creating an environment where being together with those that love them is the real value in life will be more important than ever.

Chapter 28

♦

The following excerpt is from a report by the United States Department of Labor:

OPA News Release: [05/08/2009]
Contact Name: Jennifer Kaplan
Phone Number: (202) 693-5052
Release Number: 09-0518-NAT

Statement of U.S. Labor Secretary Hilda L. Solis on April employment numbers

WASHINGTON — U.S. Secretary of Labor Hilda L. Solis issued the following statement on the April 2009 Employment Situation report released today:

"This past April, our economy lost 539,000 jobs, bringing the total number of jobs lost since this recession began to 5.7 million. The overall unemployment rate has increased to 8.9 percent.

Where are the 5.7 million unemployed workers? April of 2009's jobs losses were greater than the population of Tucson, Arizona. Millions of workers have lost their jobs over the last year, yet they rarely appear on the radar screen of most national news programs. Local news coverage had to be commended in some areas because their viewers will hold their feet to the fire if they try to ignore the obvious. There seems to be an aversion to exposing the reality of the recession to the public at large. The national mass electronic media has focused on political and entertainment stories in lieu of confronting us with images of human suffering. Is this news coverage wall intentional or a function of shallow programming?

If you listen carefully to the national reporting that is taking place in this county you may get the impression that the recession and job losses are taking place somewhere else. There is a general feeling that it is business as usual except for a few bumps in the road. Is this really the worse financial downturn since the Great Depression? During the Arab oil embargo there were visible scenes of cars line up to get rationed gas. During the summer of 2008 when gasoline prices spiked there was endless reporting from service stations with interviews of average citizens about how fuel prices were affecting their lives. There was a key difference.

High gas prices affected everyone including those that were reporting the news. It was easy to see the price of a gallon of gas while driving down the street. Employment losses such as we had during this recession occur in pockets and does not affect everyone in the same way. Your neighbor could lose their job and you may never know it happened. I think that is part of the problem with how this recession was being covered by the mass media. Where are national media centers located compared to where most people who are losing their positions? Construction and manufacturing are two areas where many have been displaced. Often there is a gulf between the blue-collar manufacturing sector and white collar world of the media. I regularly see people in business attire talking with other similarly dressed individuals about people who wear steeled toed shoes to work losing their employment.

This is not a remote and faceless recession, it is here and now. The people going through the pain are real and they have families to support. I don't think it is insensitivity causing what I view as a strange mix of reporting about a concrete problem. I just feel that whatever is going on is happening in the background. It does not take much for some warmed over personal scandals to take up all the broadcast bandwidth for days on end. Even non-stories about statements from unknown beauty queens involved in faded pageants managed to elbow their way onto the front page headlines in lieu of what seems more substantial regarding real people.

Is this the equivalent of hiding the negative side of a city so that visiting dignitaries would not witness the reality of all aspects of life? Given every report on any upward movement in the stock market or minute slowdown in unemployment claims, it would seem that the economy is on the road to recovery. Logic would dictate that job loses have to slow down at some point lest we freefall forever. Yet it seems that those who have paid the price with their livelihoods and dreams are being ignored.

We have become a scrapheap society that discards the less fortunate among us to an out of sight, out of mind status? Why isn't there a story every night highlighting the price many have paid along with the fear many feel as their time runs out? Our world of shiny distractions does not like to deal in harsh realities in deference to less substantial and more entertaining sideshows. Unemployed workers with no health insurance don't make an appealing lead in for a story.

The fourth estate of the media needs to prove that it is more than tools of the corporate parent companies that own them and shine a light on reality. Proud Americans deserve more than just being swept aside because they don't fit a feel-good programming theme.

What will it take for Americans who have been conditioned into accepting their fate in life as being largely beyond their control? What a strange stance for people whose ancestors came to this land because they refused to accept the status quo. How strange it was to see protests in other countries against bankers while here there were scant real exhibitions of public outcry. Maybe the pride of some would not allow them to show their visible emotional scars to the world. Yet still there does not seem to be a galvanizing figure to rally the dispersed souls around a single cause.

There is a constant search for a bottom to the economic downturn. Talk of a slowing in the number of people filing for unemployment benefits is one widely touted measure. What it really points out is how desensitized we have become when it relates to the real lives tied to statistics.

When Hurricane Katrina destroyed a wide area along the gulf coast of Louisiana and Mississippi there was obvious attention paid to the disaster. Much of that concern was galvanized due to the unforgettable images broadcast of the aftermath and suffering. Katrina was an event that allowed the news media to show how they could make a difference in shaping public opinion. Of course time passed and the longer term effects of the aftermath of Hurricane Katrina lost some of the grip of the immediate timeframe after the storm and coverage waned.

This is a situation of millions of newly unemployed citizens being suddenly cast into a maelstrom of uncertainty. It does not have that instant catchiness of a look-at-me story. Parents who are struggling to feed their children on a daily basis is reality television on the highest order, but it is not a feel good story.

I think it is fear that exposing the raw underbelly of what the downside really looks like will chill individuals to their core. Most people know that their time could be coming, but try to soldier on in as normal a mode as possible. The most difficult situation is a realization that the very thing to pull us out of this tailspin is for consumers to spend precious funds on goods and services. Conversely the public is pulling back and being advised to save and create emergency funds that could sustain them for 6 to 8 months in case they lose their jobs. It is easy the see how this seems to be a situation at odds with itself.

There are 2 worlds at play here, the world of commerce and the world of personal finance. Take a weekend and observe the divergent messages being sent to two different audiences. The world of commerce is focusing on measurements such as home sales figures, stock market levels and profit reports. It is often said that the key to recovery is a return of consumer spending. You will be informed of how great a time it is to acquire a home or automobile. Without ever changing channels you can get advice from noted experts in personal finance recommending that individuals cut out all unnecessary spending and amass and increase personal savings. If I am a rational thinking individual, I would be inclined to place my personal economy above that of the world of commerce. If others think as I do then we are in for a longer period of slowdown before a robust recovery comes onto the scene.

Let me be clear about one thing, I do not want the economic downturn to last any longer than necessary. I think corporate America has finally conditioned employees to look out for their personal interests above that of the company. The era of a job for life is at an end and workers now clearly understand that they are expendable resources and loyalty is often a one-way affair. How well someone does a particular job is not the issue any longer. If your task is targeted for outsourcing or elimination, it will be a sweeping decision that transcends personal competence. People will adopt an understandable opportunistic approach to work in an environment where nothing is safe including pensions, 401Ks or healthcare benefits.

Welcome to the world of the mercenary employee where maximizing the present is more important than worrying about future consequences.

Chapter 29

◆

How will we be able to recover from the
nation's greatest economic challenge since the
Great Depression? What level of pain will
people have to endure before we get back to
some level of normalcy? Those answers are
unknown. We even have the specter of a
possible global disease pandemic on the
scene. As the past fears of the deadly H5N1
bird flu had largely faded into memory
another version appeared on the landscape.
This flu did not fly but walked. H1N1, which
was also known as the swine flu, barreled
onto the stage and raised anxiety levels
worldwide. Mexico seemed to be the origin.
In addition to the health threat, was the chill a
health scare could place on economic activity.
Something on the scale of a global health
crisis could at extreme levels virtually shut
down international travel and trade. People
avoiding public gatherings and crowds could

impact already weak economic conditions. At one point Mexico City was reduced from a bustling metropolitan area to a place that resembled a ghost town at night. Citizens worldwide were seen wearing masks over their faces in order to protect themselves from exposure to the highly contagious virus. The extent to which the swine flu episode will affect our economic recovery is an issue that is difficult to gauge as it could be only a minor event or something that could come back stronger at a later time. My view on what kind of country we will be by the time this recession is over is what I will address next.

In our current situation we are a loose collection of people who live in proximity of each other. In many cities and suburban areas we really don't know our neighbors very well and that is a cause for concern as the ranks of the unemployed continues to swell. Without neighborhood connections, the question of who will be checking on each other in case of distress due to financial issues is unanswered.

The mental health of individuals experiencing stress from worries about everything from being jobless to where they will sleep each night should also be a growing concern. Children are the most exposed as their anchors are their parents, homes and routines. As more upheavals occur and children are jostled around due to family displacement for various reasons, kids will need extra attention.

At some point this economy will hit bottom and start to recover. When we emerge from this nightmare, what will we be as a country?

We must come out of this situation as one country and not continue to be a collection of special interest groups, social classes and racial subcultures. The rich and poor may not share social circles but both must recognize that they are tied together and the actions of one affect the other.

Another change that must result from this harsh lesson is a return to rational living based upon what is appropriate for your stage in life. We have been suffering from a syndrome of living in the future. That statement is not referring to some kind of time travel but instead describes the "I want it now" attitude and lifestyle. Our culture made living in the future possible with subprime mortgages, credit cards and various flexible arrangements from retailers.

I purchased my current home by using two smaller homes as stepping stones by using equity from each prior sale as down payments for each larger house. That has not been the case for the last few years as first time homeowners were moving into what formerly would have been a second or third home upgrade. Often the new homeowners would experience something called payment shock as the higher mortgage payment, utilities and upkeep took them by surprise.

The credit cards for everyone frenzy made it easy to get it all right now as acquiring those flat screen televisions, new furniture and cutting edge appliances were as easy as a swipe through the card reader. Now on to the retailers who joined in on the-future-is-now campaign with delayed payment plans. At some retailers you could take your new toy home and make no principle or interest payments for a year. The prior mindset must be banished from our landscape as we go forward.

Credit cards must become emergency use options and not a regular way of life. We must recalibrate what it means to live well. I feel we were really made to live on one income even if both people worked in a dual income household. We have used dual incomes to push our lifestyles to the limits of what both wage earners could support. The second income became the, what-do-we-want option. The problem was the luxuries we coveted created financial obligations that went far beyond the life of the desired item. There have always been situations where both spouses had jobs in order to make ends meet because of economic necessity. That is not what I am speaking of in this case. My point is if one income could support an acceptable lifestyle, then the household was far less exposed if one of the wage earners became unemployed.

I feel the one saving grace of my formative years was far less exposure to lifestyle choices I was not prepared to handle in a rational manner. What I mean is the world before 24-hour cable television did not inundate my mind with images of MTV Cribs, Top Ten Beaches and other luxurious lifestyle showcases. People tended to think, after repeated exposure to the finer things, that something was missing from their existence and they should be enjoying at least a slice of the good life. Those desires become requirements and soon action was taken to acquire the larger home, designer furniture and better vacations.

Things had changed. On a recent news program a guest was giving advice on how mixing oatmeal with certain foods could stretch the quantity. How quickly we went from talk of living the good life to discussions of how to use food extending techniques. That illustrates how fragile our economy was and how the mass media messages encouraging overconsumption placed us all at risk.

Resetting our ideals of what it means to live well will be an exercise that will cause some to require visual aids to accomplish because we have come so far from the basics of life. When I was growing up I remember when we moved from wood fired heat to natural gas. Indoor plumbing, television and a telephone were all items I can recall living without for an extended period of time. Now preteens walk around with cell phones.

What will we do to make sure this does not happen again? I will try to refrain from acting on my first impulse to acquire that new temptation unless what it is replacing is broken. I will also measure what I do by evaluating how my life would be if I did not take that action.

One thing I will always remember about my parents is they rarely bought anything on credit unless it was a major appliance after the old one died. I really reflect back on an age where people would say, "I really don't need anything" when you asked them about a gift for an upcoming occasion.

The most important change all Americans can make is to realize we are all involved in the success and failure of this country. Ruling class thinking has to come to an end. Due to the trauma caused by this latest recession, it is clear actions that seemed to take place in a vacuum brought the economy down. Hard working citizens were the people buried in the rubble of the mortgage backed security collapse. Ironically that was when the titans of corporate America discovered they would also fail if common people were not willing to spend money on their products

There is no doubt that the United States of America is still the greatest nation on earth. More dreams of the mighty and meek have been fulfilled in America than any other place on the planet. Occasionally we become lost within our prosperity and this agonizing period of economic turmoil is a painful self-correcting mechanism.

This crisis taught the country at large how to say five important words, "I really don't **need** anything."

About The Author

ESSENCE® bestselling author D.T. Pollard lives in the Dallas/Fort Worth, TX area. He is married and has one son.

He earned an academic scholarship to the School of Business and Industry at Florida A & M University. He stopped writing during his second year in college.

D T was at the top of his class in Marketing and graduated Summa Cum Laude and won the Most-Outstanding-Performance-in-Marketing award for his graduating class of 1981.

While working in sales for giants of the high-technology world for over 28 years, his desire to write returned after losing several siblings from various causes. D T Pollard is the author of Rooftop Diva - A Novel of Triumph After Katrina and Fools' Heaven – Love, Lust and Death beyond the Pulpit.

TARP Town U S A – The Recession That Saved America - takes a fresh look at the recession that emerged in 2008 and 2009.

www.DTPollard.com

Useful Information Sources

http://www.dol.gov/

http://www.fdic.gov/

http://www.whitehouse.gov/

www.ingramcontent.com/pod-product-compliance
Lightning Source LLC
Chambersburg PA
CBHW030011290326
41934CB00005B/298